WINNING RUGBY

WINNING RUGBY

COMPILED BY PAT WALSH

Macdonald
Queen Anne Press

A Queen Anne Press BOOK

First published in New Zealand in 1984 by Novalit Books,
Auckland, New Zealand

First published in Great Britain in 1985 by Queen Anne Press,
a division of Macdonald & Co (Publishers) Ltd, Maxwell House,
74 Worship Street, London EC2A 2EN
A BPCC plc Company

Jacket photograph: Colorsport

British Library Cataloguing in Publication Data

Walsh, Pat
Winning rugby.
1. Rugby football
I. Title
796.33′32 GV495

ISBN 0-356-10597-0

Additional typesetting by Hazell Watson & Viney Limited

Reproduced, printed and bound in Great Britain by
Hazell Watson & Viney Limited
Member of the BPCC Group
Aylesbury, Bucks

CONTENTS

Introduction

Many coaches and players, both young and mature, wishing to teach or improve the skills of the game of rugby, require some assistance. This book has been designed to help in that direction.

It gathers together information and ideas that the coach, player, teacher, father, mother, referee or spectator may use as he or she sees fit.

Organised coaching, where individual, unit and team skills are demonstrated and developed at a high level, should be the primary aim. The development of a basic team pattern and encouraging competence in this should be allied to simple things promoting individual flair. The immediate goal is to provide a better understanding of the game by players and a greater involvement for all concerned.

Knowledge of the simple things has to be gained in the first instance by methodical teaching. A coach must plan his work then work his plan. As he produces better equipped players he can re-organise his practice with more attention to team principles. If this procedure is followed, progress will be guaranteed, and as players move on through the grades coaches can devote time to fine tuning and providing the sophistication required at the higher levels of the game.

In accepting the position of coach of a rugby team it is important for one to understand the requirements of the job. The main function of the coach is to teach players the skills necessary to perform well in pressure situations — to teach them the how and the when. The coach should emphasize that the development of fitness and skills is a personal thing. If a coach can help the individual and the team develop a sense of pride, the players will never be satisfied with anything less than their best.

Principles of Team Play

The aim of coaching is to provide the player with knowledge and skills, in order that he may thoroughly understand the game of rugby and obtain satisfaction and enjoyment from it, whether it be at practice or at a match. The coach should develop a positive approach and appreciate the need for discipline and team work. He must clearly define his aims, objectives and teaching procedures, and must have a thorough appreciation of the game.

Irrespective of the style of game you wish to play, the brilliant individuals you may have, or the tactics you intend to use, you must have certain basic principles to refer to and apply.

The five principles are:

- move forward
- support the ball carrier
- back up
- apply constant pressure
- be positive.

The first principle is to **move forward**. This applies to everyone in the team, irrespective of his position. A forward chasing the kick-off, a fullback joining the backline, any player with ball in hand, or in support of the ball carrier, must at all times be aiming to move forward.

Secondly, the ball carrier must be supported. The player with ball in hand must feel confident that he has **support**. It is good to know that all you have to do when you have the ball in hand is to run hard or drive forward and there will always be someone close by.

The third principle is the **back-up**, to maintain continuity. Running, passing and backing up are important if the team is to keep moving forward. In the case of forwards, this can involve passing from the hip at close quarters, or during a tackle, releasing the ball to another player in support of the ball carrier.

Fourthly, **constant pressure** must be exerted upon the opposition by running hard, backing up and tackling effectively. Constant pressure *causes* something to happen, and this is better than *waiting* for it to happen. Denying the opposition time and space will reduce the options available to them and force them into errors. It is a well-known saying that the side that makes the least mistakes usually wins.

Finally, a positive mental attitude is vital:

Life's battle doesn't always go to the
Biggest or strongest or fastest man,
But sooner or later the fellow who wins
Is the fellow who thinks he can.

To **move forward** we must be physically fit, and special individual training programmes apart from normal team sessions are important. To support the ball carrier we must be fit enough to move swiftly into position. We must want to work as hard without the ball as we do with it, and when we get the ball in hand we must explode and surge again.

Speed and anticipation will help players get into good positions of **support for the ball carrier** and will allow constant back-up. We will need to be able to catch, pass, kick and tackle as we continue to **back up** in our efforts to reach the opposition goal-line. Our ability to swerve, fend, side-step, change pace and be generally elusive will help us to maintain **pressure on our opponents**. In some cases we must take the tackle, and here we must aim to keep on our feet, making sure that the ball is always readily available for our support players. In most of these situations individual skills are paramount and are the basis of sound unit development and teamwork skills.

Although there is no such thing as over-coaching, coach domination can have a destructive effect on the game. It is necessary to develop players' skills so they have options, and to teach them to think about when to use their options. Players must be allowed flexibility on the field to attack or defend according to opportunity.

The functions of the coach is to help players:

- obtain maximum satisfaction and enjoyment from the game in matches, practices and training
- develop a positive approach and recognise the need for teamwork
- develop individual skills through constant practice so that they can better carry out the five parts of the team contract, to which they have committed themselves.

Move forward, support the ball carrier, back up, apply constant pressure, be positive.

Photo shows a good body position of the ball carrier and depth in support of him.

It is easier to attack in the right direction if you get the ball as you move forward. Primary possession comes from the set plays, the scrum and the lineout, and therefore quality ball must be achieved. A solid scrum at your put-ins and controlled deliveries from your lineouts are essential. There is no reason why a team achieving good ball as it moves forward should not reach the advantage line every time.

Attention to good body position and total physical commitment help us to engage the opposition and to develop the move forward. Straightening as we are running forward is also vital. From set play this is mainly the role of the second five-eighth or centre, as the insides are usually preoccupied with creating space for him to do so, while those outside are awaiting development. To support the ball carrier we must position ourselves with sufficient depth so that we can run onto the ball.

Back up with the positive thought that you want to take a pass and ensure the continuity of the ball on the move forward, and are not just backing up to cover an error. We pass the ball on to a support player who is under less pressure and who will straighten the attack before passing to a back-up player.

Constant pressure, which destroys the quality of opposition ball, and solid tackling where the opposition goes to ground are key factors. Even though a ball may be lost, it is essential to contest it to the very end. We must force the opposition ball carrier to make a quick decision, thereby reducing his options: don't allow them to come to us, but rather we should move forward and put pressure on them.

In each game or practice we must be positive in our

approach, and develop and encourage certain skills and qualities, for example, kicking to an area where possession can be regained, staying on your feet, re-distributing the ball, aggressive tackling and explosive running.

Success gives a player a feeling of confidence, so early practices must be within the capabilities of the players. A careful progression from basic to more advanced skills will lead to success, self-assurance, and personal satisfaction and enjoyment.

Rugby, a dynamic sport played by aspiring eight-year-olds and seasoned players alike, is constantly changing as laws are refined, styles streamlined and methods improved. This book is a contribution to the development of this mighty game.

A dynamic sport played by young and old alike.

Fitness for Rugby

Total all-round fitness for rugby means the progressive development of all the following physical qualities:

Stamina — the ability to persist at a physically tiring pace.
Skill — the ability to perform a physical activity with ease and efficiency.
Speed — the ability to increase the rate of movement over distance.
Strength — the ability of a muscle to apply force against resistance.
Suppleness — the ability to take a joint through its full range of movement.

Careful conditioning will delay the onset of fatigue in a player and thereby enable him to maintain a high rate of performance over a longer period of time. This in turn enhances his enjoyment of the game and benefits play overall. The essence of any training programme should be recovery, work and rest, work and rest.

Fitness demands will vary according to the time of the year and the grade of your team. The rugby year can be divided into three distinct parts.

Post-Season

Maintenance of good physical condition in the 'off' season, maybe 8 to 10 weeks.

Running — three or four times weekly to maintain stamina, varying times from 20 minutes to 45 minutes. Use the out and back run, which easily identifies progress. When running for stamina, seek to reduce time from ten to eight minutes per mile.

Weight training — with moderate weight resistance to build up strength. No more than six exercises. Start at three sets of 12 repetitions. Gradually build to four sets of 15 repetitions. Two or three times weekly — develop quantity.

1. Bicep Curl (15 kg)
2. Sit-Ups
3. Press Behind Neck (15 kg)
4. Front Squat (25 kg)
5. Standing Rows (15 kg)
6. Power Clean (20 kg)

These exercises and starting totals are only guidelines. Contact local physical education staff for expert opinion.

Circuit training — Two or three times weekly.

1. Press-Ups (10)
2. Sit-Ups (10)
3. Back Lifts (10)
4. Bouncing Split Squats (10)
5. Pull-Ups (3)
6. Squat Thrusts (10)

Except for Pull-Ups (two to four total), you do 10 repetitions on each exercise. Start on three lots of 10 repetitions per exercise, moving from press ups through to squat thrusts and then back to press ups again. Start with three circuits, then build up to 10.

Pre-Season

Transition from a large volume to more intense work, say 6 to 8 weeks.

Running — Twice weekly, do 10 lots of 100-metre sprints in 14-16 seconds with a 90-second recovery, building to 20 lots. Then switch to 8 × 200-metre runs in 32-36 seconds with 2½ minutes recovery, build to 12 × 200 metres. Run this only twice weekly and stretch thoroughly first. It is wise to continue distance running once or twice weekly.

Weight training — with heavy resistance. Switch from quantity work to quality by increasing the weight, and decreasing sets and repetitions to three sets of 10, two to three times weekly.

Circuit training — Continue earlier exercises, reducing repetitions for the lower and younger grades.

A univarsally favourite exercise — press-ups!

Playing Season

The eight months of the playing season is the time for skill and technique training plus team patterns and team training. Training should include at least one distance run, along with one or two weight or circuit sessions. The emphasis during these sessions should be on maintaining the fitness levels built up during the first two stages.

Post Season

Development of work volume

Distance running

Moderate strength work

Circuit training

Pre-Season

Increase in intensity

Interval running

Heavy strength work

Maintenance of circuits

Some distance running

Playing Season

Skill, technique and team training

Combination of interval and distance running

Maintenance of strength

Continuation of circuits

Shuttle runs

Variety in training is also important, and swimming, cycling, tennis, badminton and squash add interest to a training regime.

Limbering up is important — and it can be fun!

Before suggesting a training schedule for team coaches to use on team training nights, it is important to consider the demands of the game. Studies show that of 80 minutes playing time in top club games, there are only 27 minutes when the ball is in play. It is also interesting to note that a player on average has the ball in his hands for no longer than a minute in a game. Analysis of running patterns shows that forwards cover approximately 6000 metres, while backs average 4000 metres. Forwards cover 33 per cent of the distance at top speed and the rest at three-quarter pace, while backs cover 50 per cent at top pace and 50 per cent at three-quarter pace.

We should aim for 2000 to 3000 metres fitness running per session. It is as well to structure running sessions at a work:rest ratio of 1:2, and not to neglect team techniques at lineouts, scrums, mauls and kick-offs, both on attack and defence.

Running — The rugby field lends itself to easily organised running training with its halfway and 22 line divisions along with the sideline/goal-line perimeter for laps and relays. Standard flags or cones can be used if required for clearer markings.

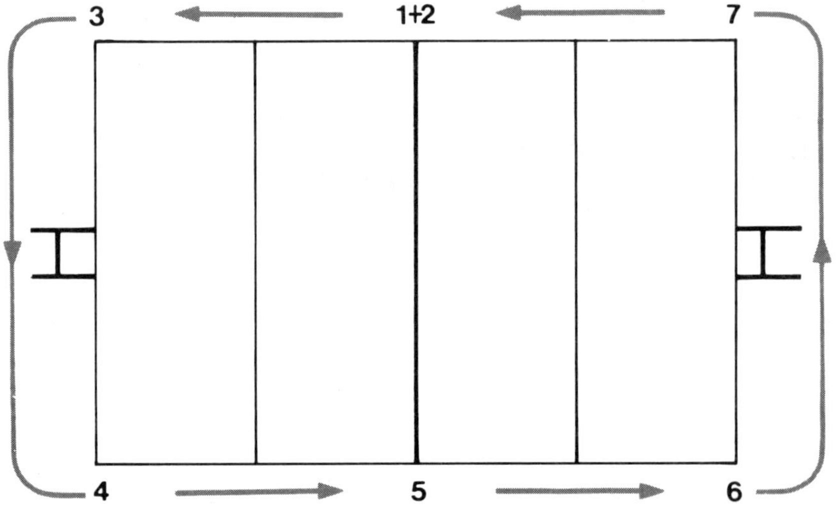

Continuous Relay — No. 1 and No. 2 on halfway. Player at each corner and opposite halfway line. On 'go' 1 runs to 3 carrying a football, 3 runs to 4, and so on around the field. Two or three groups could work at this.

- Set a time or distance target; first No. 1 back home or 6-8 minutes run. 12 laps of the field are approx. 3000 metres.

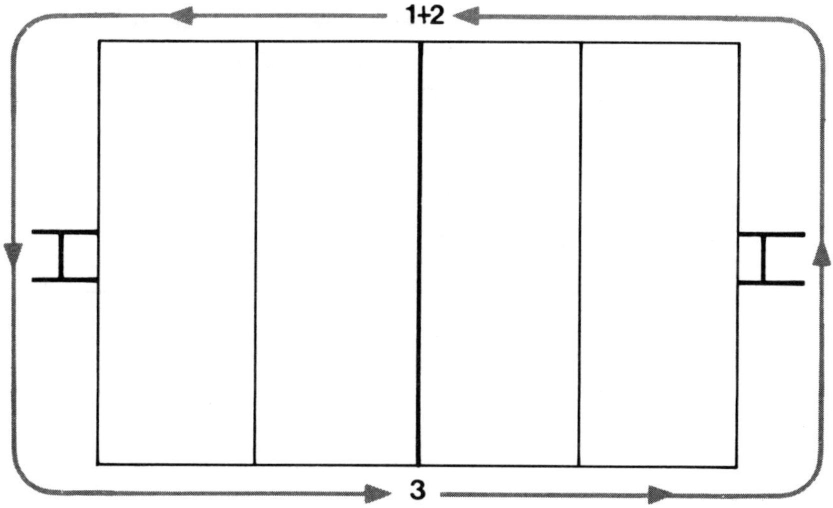

Three-Man Relay — No. 1 in position at halfway. On 'go' he carries football to No. 3 position and stays there. No. 3 runs to meet No. 2, who runs to meet No. 1.

• Again set a time or distance target. Build up number of laps gradually.

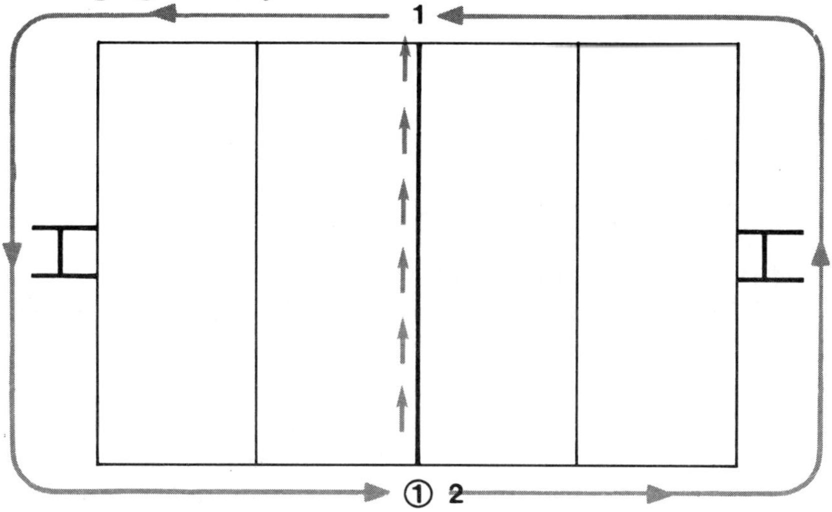

Two-Man Relay (see over)

Two-Man Relay — No. 1 in possession. On 'go' he runs around field to where No. 2 is waiting. No. 1 passes to No. 2, who in turn runs around. No. 1 now has to cross field to his original position to receive from No. 2 and continue.

• Again set a time or distance target. Any number of pairs can participate.

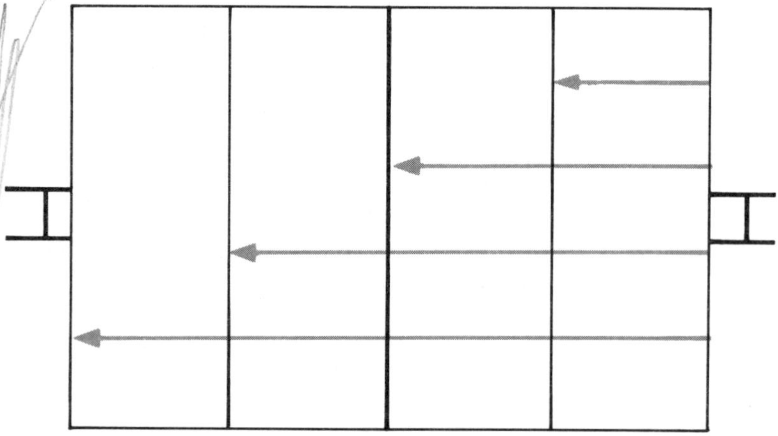

Pyramid Runs — Stand on goal-line. Sprint to near 22 m line. Wind down and walk back. Sprint to halfway, jog back. Sprint from goal-line to far 22 m line, then jog back. Sprint from goal-line to goal-line. This pyramid totals 250 metres. Repeat giving a total of 500 metres. Allow a recovery jog, then repeat according to the fitness levels of the players.

• For variation aim for 10 × 50 metres or 20 × 25 metres as a team relay.

'Pinetree' Special — Three groupings of 'tight five', 'loosies' and 'halfbacks', and 'rest of backs'. Begin from corner flag. Run around and through far goalpost

and return to finish at opposite goalpost. Wind down by jogging a full lap of field. Players remember own times.

- Repeat again during and towards end of session. A test of stamina.

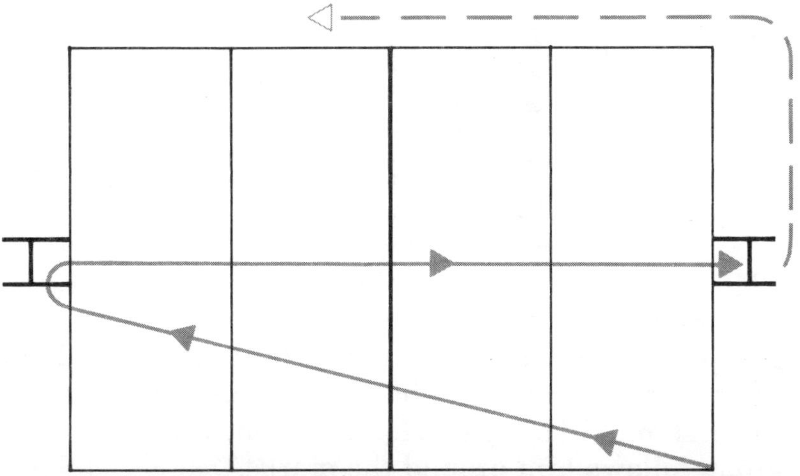

Wear warm clothing while limbering up in preparation for training.

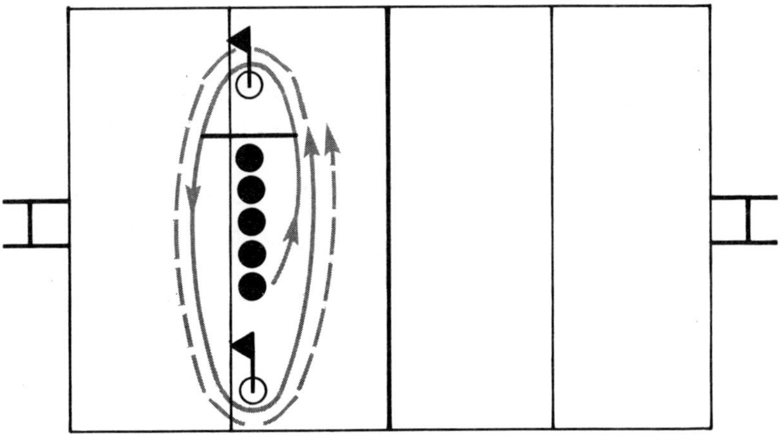

Chase the Tail — Groups lined up in files, markers placed about 5-10 metres in front of and behind each group. Last man (alone) runs past his team around the front mark, then around back mark, and as he passes the first man in his group for the second time the whole group follows him around the marks.

• Repeat until all the members of the team have had turns as leader.

With these ideas and a little forward planning, coaches can devise several relays which can be varied with pick up and carry, hopping, change direction, sprint and jogging, and long line with last to front.

Fitness Tests — When dealing with a squad of 18-20 players, keep the tests to the point and make them relevant. Relate all times and personal scores to the player. Fitness is a personal thing, and players should be encouraged to note their own progress and to make comparisons. Test once a month for running stamina and running speed, using one test on one night and the second on another. Other tests can be run if time allows.

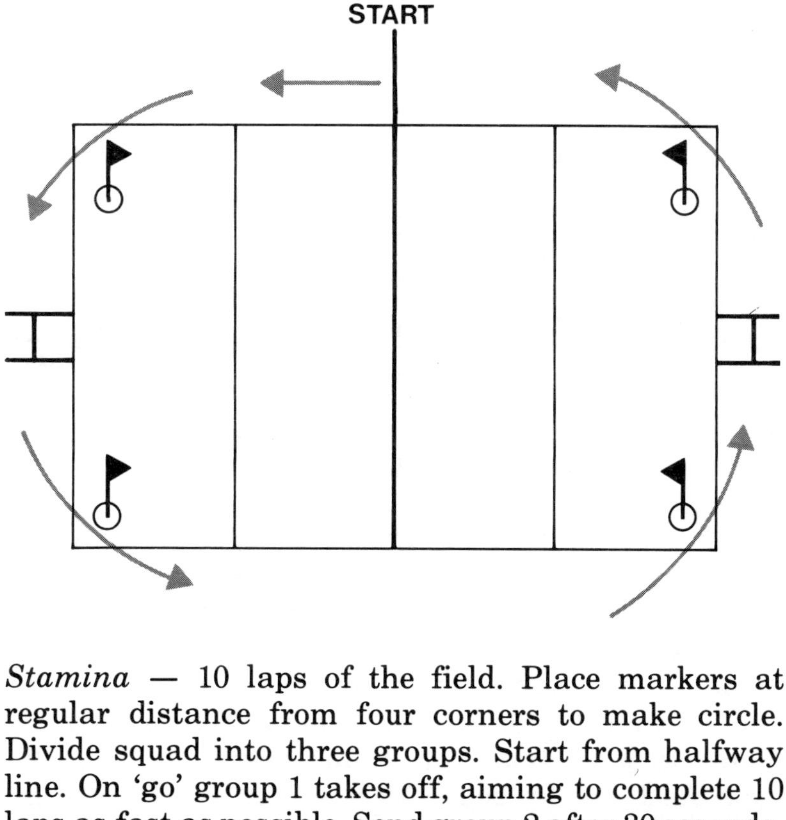

Stamina — 10 laps of the field. Place markers at regular distance from four corners to make circle. Divide squad into three groups. Start from halfway line. On 'go' group 1 takes off, aiming to complete 10 laps as fast as possible. Send group 2 after 30 seconds, group 3 after 60 seconds. This helps to spread the group out, get the 'slowies' away to a good start, and avoid congestion. As each group finishes, call out time in minutes and seconds as they run past. Record on a sheet of paper.

• Aim to get within 5-10 seconds of fastest time. This is a good way to maintain stamina.

Dr K. D. Cooper's 12-minute walk/run test is a measure of general endurance. Each player runs for 12 minutes at his own pace. The aim is to cover as much distance as possible. Distance is recorded. As a guide, 10 laps of a rugby field in 12 minutes is considered very good.

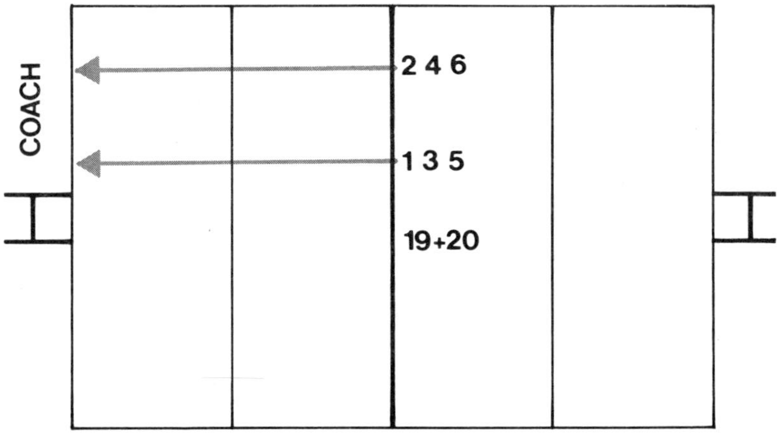

Speed — Distance halfway to goal-line. Players stand in pairs on halfway line facing goal-line where coach is standing with a stop-watch in each hand. Players 19 and 20, who run last, are responsible for starting the pairs. On 'go' 1 and 2 sprint hard towards coach, who calls out times for each. All have three attempts and the fastest time is recorded for each.

- Again times are personal and should be better than, but at least comparable to, earlier tests. A fair time is 6.8-7.6 seconds over 50 metres.

Strength — Pull-Ups, for upper body strength. Start with arms straight, feet off floor, hands shoulder width apart, palms facing forward over bar. Bend arms to pull chin above height of bar. Arms are then straightened. This is one pull up. Continue as many times as possible. Average 5-8.

Squat (Sargent) Jumps. A test of explosive strength valuable for backs (for immediate explosiveness from inert standing) and forwards (during lineouts, kick-offs). The idea is to jump upwards as high as possible.

Muscular Endurance and Strength
Press-Ups for arm and shoulder region. Press-ups can be timed over 30 seconds with the following standards:
Excellent — 32
Very Good — 29
Average — 25
Fair — 21

Sit-Ups in pairs for the abdominal region. Standards, timed over 30 seconds, are as follows:
Excellent — 30
Very Good — 26
Average — 22
Fair — 19

Step-Ups for the legs. Over 30 seconds standard times are:
Excellent — 30
Very Good — 28
Average — 26
Fair — 22

Results of these tests provide a general fitness profile for each player. For individual players in any team, the results will vary according to the player's position, the specific job required, and the attitude. The coach should use these results to encourage more effort and better fitness — even healthy competition among players. Tests after a heavy social weekend will definitely show poorer results than those recorded later in the week.
Remember: train don't strain.

Sit ups with knees bent. The coach uses a stopwatch to time the exercise.

Warm-up exercises

When considering the warm-up exercises, we usually associate the common calisthenic exercises to be sufficient; however, we feel that stretching is more important. Proper stretching will prevent muscle tears from the tendinous attachments, and enable the performer to exercise vigorously with less fear of injury.

The following changes take place in the body after a proper warm-up period:

- Temperature increases throughout the body, allowing the muscles to contract and relax with greater speed. The temperature increases also causes increase in metabolic rate.
- Blood flow is increased to the muscles due to blood vessel dilation.

Any space at all can be used for stretching exercises.

- With increased blood flow, oxygen supply is also increased.
- Heart rate, blood pressure, respiratory rate are also increased and more energy producing nutrients are carried to the muscles and waste products are eliminated faster.
- Temperature rise in active muscles.

Following is a basic set of warm-up exercises. Careful attention should be given to their proper execution.

1. Hamstring Stretch
While standing erect, cross one foot over the other with the heel of the crossed heel up. This keeps the pelvis straight. Reach down toward the ground twice on a slow 1-2 count and on a count of 3, touch the ground. Do this 10 times, then cross the other leg and repeat 10 times.

2. Quadricep Stretch
Kneel with toes pointed away from the body in back of you. Place hands on your arches in back of you and lean backward, at the same time raising the pelvis up and out. You can feel the stretch in the quadriceps. Repeat 20 times.

START ACTION

3. Low Back Twister

Bend forward at the waist with legs spread past shoulder width. Bend the arms at the elbow keeping the forearm parallel to the ground. With a wide sweeping motion of the arms left-right rotate the trunk forcefully stretching the low back. Repeat 50 times.

START ACTION

4. Abdominal Twister

Lie on your back on the floor, place hands behind the head, pull knees up toward chest and raise head toward the knees in a cradle position. Touch right elbow to left knee, then left elbow to right knee. Alternate as fast as possible. Build up to 100 reps.

START ACTION FINISH

5. Caterpillar Push-up

Bend forward placing hands about a metre from your feet. Lower your chest and shoulders toward floor, arch back, drive forward raising head and shoulders and extend arms straight.

START ACTION

6. Trunk Rotations
Stand with feet shoulder width apart, bend knees, and place hands with fingers interlocked behind head. Bend forward at the waist and touch right elbow to right knee, rotate the trunk to the right and then bend backwards forcing the hips forward, continue rotating trunk and touch left elbow to left knee (to the side) and continue to starting position bending forward with both elbows touching both knees. Alternate directions to avoid dizziness.

Stretching and suppleness

Stretching exercises to be done before and after the game (to take approximately 10 minutes). Each stretch is to be held for (10 + 20) 30 seconds unless otherwise specified.

One of the most important and least understood areas of athlete conditioning is stretching, a series of manoeuvres involving the nerves, muscles and blood vessels, and designed to alert the body to impending activity and to protect joints and their associated muscles, ligaments and tendons from injury by increasing their flexibility. Personal programmes have been developed for hundreds of athletes, including sprinters and long-distance runners, rugby, soccer, tennis and basketball players, wrestlers, swimmers and skiers. In each case, other factors being equal, injuries have been dramatically reduced.

If professional athletes rely on stretching to prevent injuries, then all rugby coaches should be promoting proper stretching procedures as a matter of course. Stretching is free, requires no equipment, demands a minimum of time, can be performed under most conditions, and it works.

Stretching aids in various ways:

- The athlete develops an awareness of the muscles being stretched, resulting in better control.
- The volume and speed of nerve impulse transmission and the athlete's response rate are increased.
- The blood supply to connective tissue, especially ligaments and tendons, is increased, and muscle tension is reduced.
- Increased flexibility of joints.
- After vigorous activity muscle tissue remains partially contracted for up to 48 hours; muscles are shorter and lose their elasticity, resulting in stiffness and soreness. After-game stretching will help overcome this problem.

Static stretching, selective and pertinent to the athlete's sport, should be performed carefully, with the athlete concentrating and giving his full attention to the area involved. This is to prevent the initiation of the 'stretch-reflex', which produces muscle tension, negating the objective of stretching. When the correct posture has been assumed the athlete should slowly lengthen the appropriate group until the initial stretch is felt, holding for 10 seconds and then increasing the stretch slightly for another 10 to 20 seconds. Shorter periods are stipulated by some authorities, but in our

7

2

6

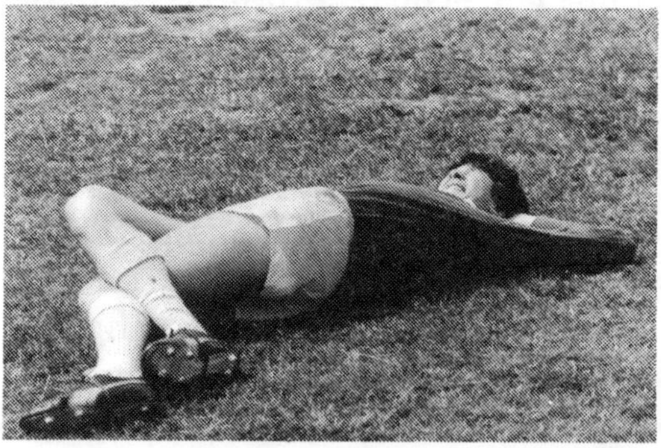

12

Stretching exercises (see pp 38–43)

experience they are less productive. Each routine is therefore divided into two parts.

- Initial stretch.
- Full stretch or 'productive' period.

N.B. Do not 'pump' or move during stretching, as this will increase connective tissue tension; of course this does not apply to the ankle rotation sequence.

Be Careful........Stretching must be applied slowly.

Be Subjective.....Ignore your team-mate's ability. Stretching is an individual quality.

Be Methodical....Complete each stretch before attempting the next.

Be Objective......Note the increased flexibility achieved from week to week.

Be Regular.......Develop the stretching habit morning and night, as well as before and after practice and/or games.

There are hundreds of stretching activities involving all body areas. The following series (next page) is ideally suited to the rugby athlete but is by no means exhaustive, and individuals are encouraged to develop their own routines, especially for poor flexibility.

1. Reach for the left shoulder blade with the right hand, fingers outstretched, using the left hand as a stabiliser in front of the right elbow. This will stretch the lateral trunk, shoulder and arm muscles to the elbow. Repeat with the left arm.

2. With the fingers interlaced and palms facing upwards, reach away as far as possible. This stretches the trunk, shoulders, arms and, to a lesser extent, the legs.

3. Stand with feet comfortably apart, arms loosely at the sides and knees partially bent. This may require a shift in your centre of gravity but, executed properly, will stretch the large muscle groups at the front of the thighs (quadriceps).

4. Retain the knee-bent posture from the previous exercise and drop forward, allowing the arms to hang loosely, thereby stretching the posterior thigh muscles (hamstrings) and the buttocks.

5. Grasp the right leg (above the ankle) with the right hand pulling the leg towards you from the hip as an unit. Very slowly rotate the foot, first clockwise and then anti-clockwise, 10 times. This is best done by grasping the toes with the free hand and imagining that the toes are inscribing a circle. While this is non-static, it is the finest stretch for ankle ligaments, especially for athletes with weakness in this area. Keep the extended foot upright and the knee slightly bent. Repeat with the left ankle.

6. Assume the seated posture with soles together, grasping the toes with both hands and pulling the heels as close as possible towards the crotch. Be careful to bend forward from the hips, keeping the back straight and ensuring that the elbows are in front of the shins. This stretches the hips generally, but primarily the inner thigh and crotch areas.

15 seconds
each arm

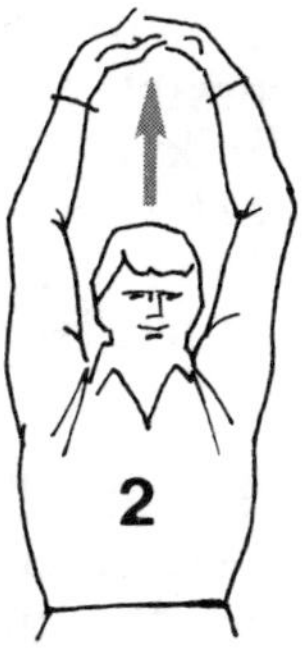

10 seconds

30 seconds

30 seconds

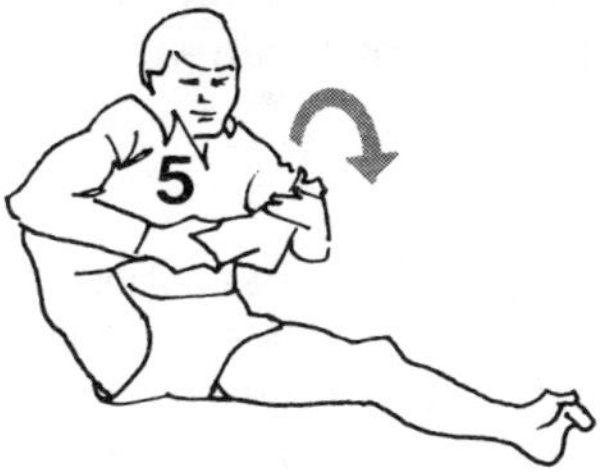

15 times
each direction

30 seconds

7. With the right knee bent, place the right foot as close as possible to the buttock, thus placing a minimum of strain on the knee. Place the left sole inside the right thigh and lean backwards onto both hands with the arms outstretched. This is an excellent stretch for the front thigh muscles. Repeat with the left leg.

8. With the left leg outstretched, foot upright, bend the right knee, placing the right foot inside the left upper thigh. Bend forward, again from the hips, reaching as far as possible towards the ankle. This is a multiple stretch especially good for the hamstring group. Do not drop the head. Repeat with the right leg.

9. With the legs wide apart, keep the back straight and bend forwards from the hips, reaching out with both hands for stability. This is a good bilateral groin, thigh and buttock stretch.

10. Simply a repetition of number six. Reduce the time to 20 seconds and observe the increase in your ability to stretch!

11. Lie flat on your back with the knees bent, feet comfortably apart and fingers interlaced behind the head at ear level. Pull up the head, tucking the chin into the chest to stretch the muscles from the base of the skull to between the shoulder blades. Hold for eight seconds and repeat three times.

12. Using the starting position for the previous exercise and keeping the shoulder blades flat on the floor, cross the left leg over the right just above the knee. Use the left leg as a lever to pull the right knee towards the floor. This is an excellent manoeuvre for anyone with a lower back problem and creates a stretch from the right armpit through the lateral rib, lower spine, hip and thigh areas to the knee. Repeat with the left leg.

30 seconds
each leg

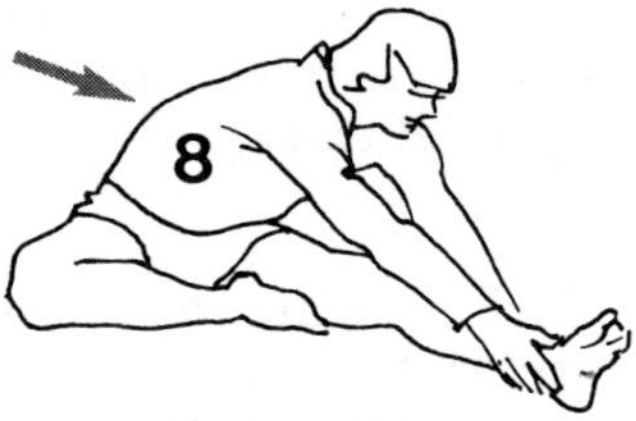

30 seconds
each leg

30 seconds

20 seconds

3 times
5 seconds each

20 seconds
each side

13. Lie on the back with arms and legs outstretched. The objective is to reach away, making the body as thin as possible. Breathe normally and use three repetitions lasting eight seconds each.

14. On the hands and knees with the thumbs pointing outwards, move the trunk slightly backwards. This is an excellent stretch for the wrist and arms.

15. Following on from the previous stretch, place your forehead on the left forearm. Pull back with the outstretched arm to stretch the arm, shoulder, side and back muscles. Repeat with the left arm.

16. Using the starting crouch, arms outstretched and right toes level with the left knee, move the trunk forward carefully to stretch the right achilles tendon. It is difficult for most athletes to keep the heel flat, but do your best. Repeat with the left leg.

17. With your trunk forward over the bent right knee, extend the left leg with the bent knee some inches off the floor. Drop the pelvis to create a stretch on the ileo-psoas muscle running from the pelvis to the inner thigh. Repeat with the other leg.

18. Finish off with the familiar squat to stretch the lower back and leg. Keep the arms between the legs and do not worry if you are unable to keep the heels flat.

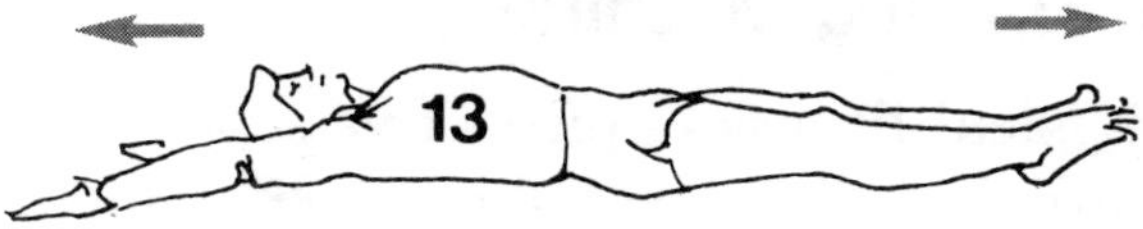

3 times
5 seconds each

20 seconds

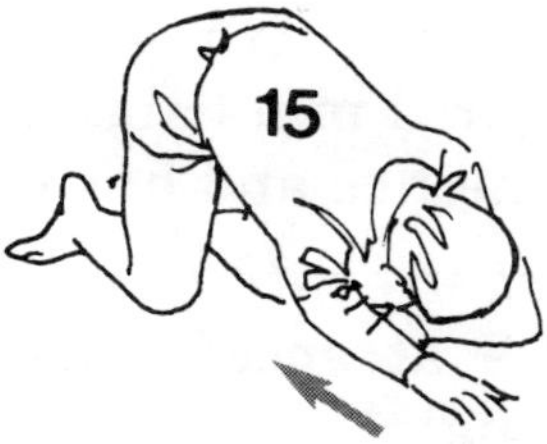

10 seconds
each arm

10 seconds
each leg

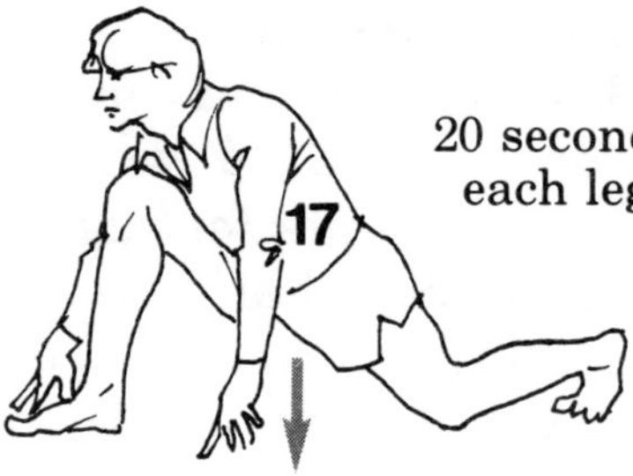

20 seconds
each leg

20 seconds

Weight Training Machine

Total physical fitness requires five separate components — stamina, speed, suppleness, skill and strength — and every rugby player should realise the value of strength training as part of his physical make-up for the season. The best way to build up strength is through progressive resistance exercises, gradually overloading the muscles to produce the desired effect.

Strength can be sub-divided into three main groups:

Gross strength — this is maximum strength and is not required in its absolute form as it is closely related to isometrics and has little movement.

Fast strength (power) — this is the ability to produce force at speed and is often referred to as 'elastic strength'.

Endurance strength — this is the ability to maintain the quality of the muscular contraction over a period of time.

For rugby, in particular, a balance between fast strength and endurance strength is required as assistance exercise.

Progressive resistance exercises have until recently been mostly associated with free weight-training with barbells and dumbells. However, a far more convenient way of training is on a fixed weight machine. Its advantages over free weights for rugby players are many. It takes less space than several barbell stations; there is no mess from loose discs or collars being strewn around; the danger factor in weight training is eliminated as all weights are on a central stem and supporters are not needed.

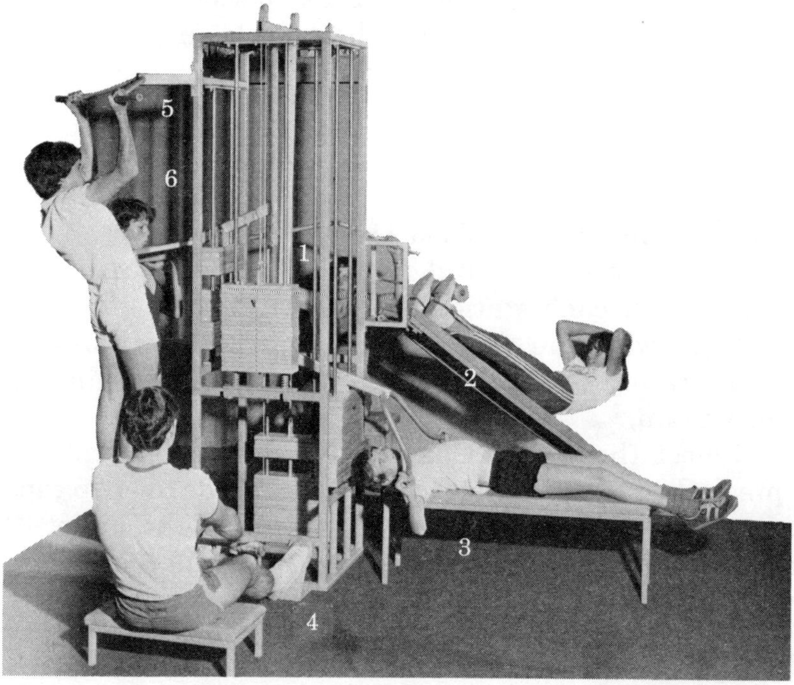

Fixed Weight Trainer — 6 stations: 1. Press /latt station (arms); 2. Abdominal conditioner (stomach); 3. Bench press (shoulders); 4. Rowing conditioner (back); 5. Chin-ups (back and shoulders); 6. Shoulder and squat station (legs).

Further, there is no danger of floor damage and time normally spent taking off and putting on extra weights in a bar is eliminated.

The stations have complete versatility, each offering several exercise variations. Charts or personal scorecards can be used to check progression through the season and properly organised, a team can have a thorough strength workout in 25-35 minutes, either before or after team training.

Used gradually over a brief period, Multi-Line Weight Trainers can pack solid muscle on players and ensure a better physique for all users.

Exercising for the first time

1. Choose a circuit and find the diagrams showing exercise for each station.

2. Start with one set of no more than 25 repetitions on each station (except for chin-ups, where you aim for maximum).

3. Select the weights as suggested and perform the prescribed repetitions. As a general guide over 25 reps on one exercise means the weight is too light, under 10 reps on one exercise means the weight is too heavy. Plates weight 5 kg and 7 kg (larger). The adjust weight, pull out selector pin and place in hole opposite weight to suit.

4. Having performed the set of exercises at each station means you have completed a circuit, or set of exercises.

Circuit progress

1. Progess should be gradual over a long period of time. It is important to keep correct form in all exercises.

2. Aim for three sessions per week for progress. Two will maintain a strength level, one is not enough.

3. Begin with one circuit. After two weeks progess to

two circuits. After four to six weeks, try three circuits. This will vary according to how regular a user you become.

Progress should follow along these lines for beginners:

Circuit	**No.**	**First Time**		**2-3 Weeks**		**4-6 Weeks**			**2-3 Months**		
			One Circuit	*Two Circuits*		*Three Circuits*					
Station	*No:*		*Weight*	*Reps*		*Reps*					
Latts	1	15kg	25	25	14	25	25	9	25	25	25
Abdo	2	—	15	15	9	25	25	8	25	25	25
Press	3	30kg	25	25	16	25	25	10	25	25	25
Rows	5	15kg	25	25	11	25	25	18	25	25	25
Chins	4	—	max.	max.	max.	8	5	2	8	8	8
Squats	6	35kg	25	25	19	25	25	12	25	25	25

On reaching this point the trainer can either (a) Increase the weight; (b) Set time limits; (c) Switch to another circuit. See circuit tables following:

CIRCUIT 1

Station	*Exercise*	*Muscle Groups*
1	Kneeling, pull to rear neck.	Trapezius; latissimus dorsi.
2	Bent knee sit-ups.	Abdominals.
3	Bench press.	Pectorals; triceps.
4	Standing up rowing.	Rear deltoid; trapezius.
5	Undergrip chin-ups	Biceps; front deltoid.
6	Back squats.	Quadriceps; gluteals.

CIRCUIT 2

Station	*Exercise*	*Muscle Groups*
1	Triceps press down.	Triceps.
2	Knee raises.	Abdominals.
3	Kneeling front press.	Front deltoids; triceps.
4	Bent over rowing.	Trapezius; latissimus dorsi.
5	Overgrip chins.	Biceps; latissimus dorsi.
6	Front squats.	Quadriceps.

CIRCUIT 1

CIRCUIT 2

CIRCUIT 3

Station	*Exercise*	*Muscle Groups*
1	Kneeling pull to chest.	Trapezius; latissimus dorsi.
2	Sit-ups with twist.	Abdominals; external obliques.
3	Kneeling press behind neck.	Deltoid; trapezius; triceps.
4	Biceps curl.	Biceps.
5	Knee raises	Abdominals.
6	Heel raises.	Gastrocnemius.

CIRCUIT 4

Station	*Exercise*	*Muscle Groups*
1	Kneeling undergrip, pull to head.	Biceps
2	Leg raises.	Abdominals.
3	Dead lift.	Quads; gluteals.
4	Neck curls.	Upper trapezius.
5	Hip flexors (straight legs).	Abdominals.
6.	Jerk.	Triceps; deltoids (thighs).

CIRCUIT 3

CIRCUIT 4

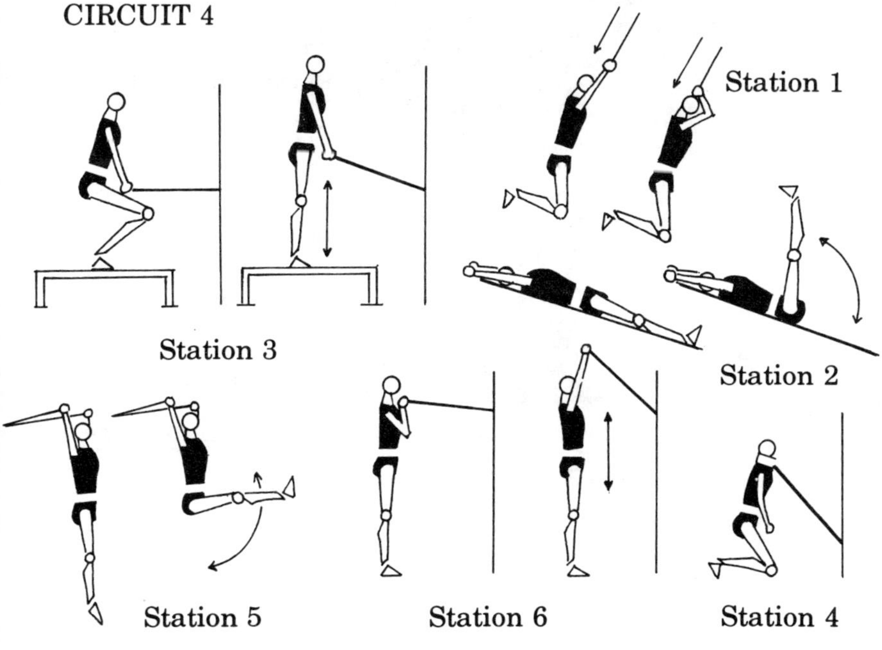

Body muscle chart

These diagrams illustrate and name the major muscles and muscle groups. This chart may be particularly helpful if you wish to isolate and condition a specific area of weakness. Listed in each muscle group is a series of exercises affecting these specific groups.

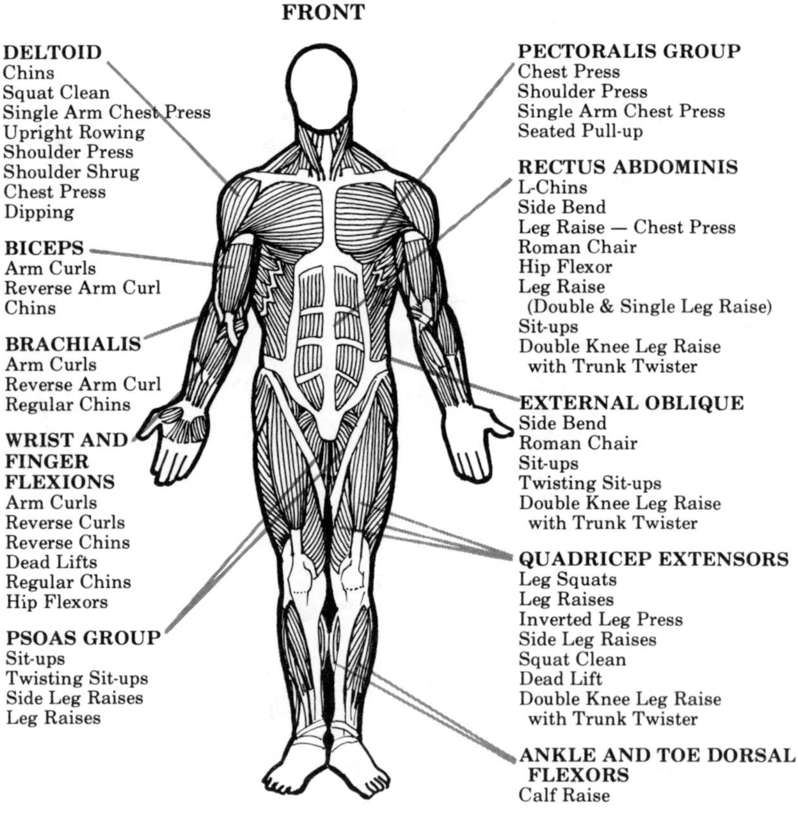

BACK

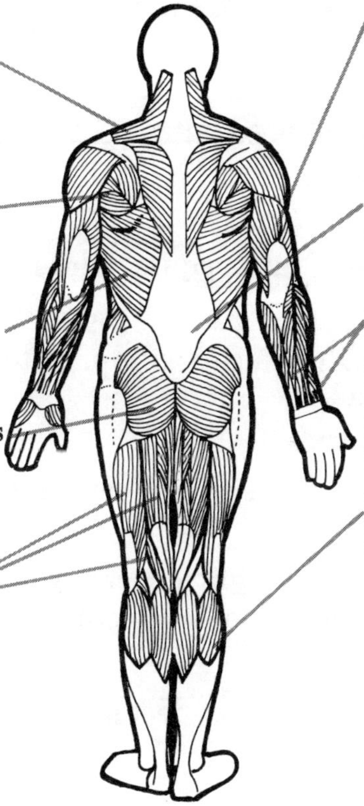
TRAPEZIUS
Dipping
Squat Clean
Shoulder Shrug
Reverse Shoulder Press
Dead Lift
Chins
Upright Rowing
TERES MAJOR
Dipping
Chins
Bent Rowing
Upright Rowing
LATISSIMUS DORSI
Bent Rowing
Dipping
Chins
GLUTEUS MAXIMUS
Leg Squats
Back Leg Raises
Side Leg Raises
Dead Lift
Squat Clean
Inverted Leg Press
HAMSTRINGS
Leg Squats
Inverted Leg Press
TRICEPS
Squat Clean
Single Arm Chest Press
Shoulder Press
Chest Press
French Curl
Dipping
Chins
SACROSPINALES
Back Arch
Back Leg Raises
Dead Lifts
Squat Clean
WRIST AND FINGER EXTENSORS
Arm Curls
Reverse Chins
Reverse Curls
Regular Chins
Dead Lifts
Hip Flexors
CALF (GASTROCNEMIUS)
Calf Raises

General Stretching and Strengthening Activity

General Body Movements (G.B.M.s)

Individual

Squat Thrusts — Stand, squat, thrust, squat, stand.

Mark Time — Push-up position. Alternate hand to chest or forehead.

Pistons — Push-up position. Feet forward and back.

Push-Ups — Back straight, chest lower and raise. Vary with a clap hands as you straighten.

Circle Hand-Walk — Keep feet on spot, step sideways on hands.

Sit-Ups — Knees bent, elbows to knees. Vary position of hands.

Heels Raise — On back, heels raise, hold, lower.

Squat thrusts.

Mark time.

Pistons.

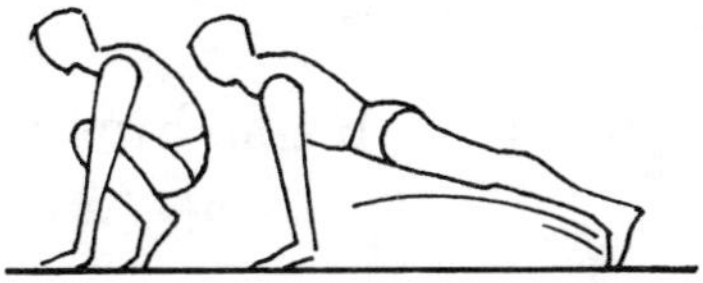

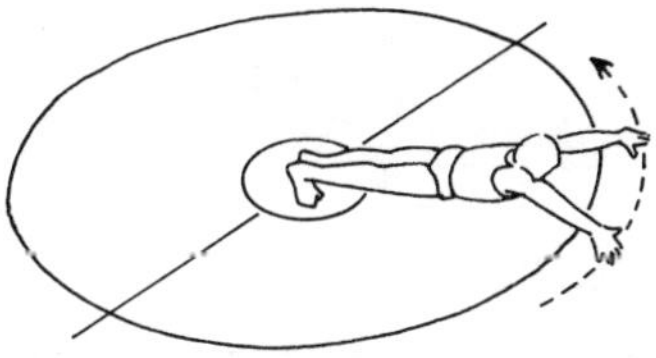

Circle hand-walk.

Push-ups.

Heels raise.

Sit-up.

V-Sit — Hold, bend and stretch legs alternately, pump arms whilst feet off ground.

Step-Ups — On and off low height.

Run on the Spot — Pump arms and legs. 30 seconds, 1 minute, 2 minutes.

Leg Signals — Side balance, raise arm, raise leg, arm and leg together.

Hip Lift — Raise hips as high as possible and lower.

Pairs

Two-Handed Tug of War — Partners face, clasp hands, using finger grip or wrist grip.

One-Handed Tug of War — Partners grip right (left) wrists, turn sideways, outer border of near foot touches partner's.

Duck Fighting — Partners face, clasp hands behind back and bend knees fully. Taking little jumps from this position, each tries to over-balance the other by bumping shoulder to shoulder, palms to palms.

V-sit.

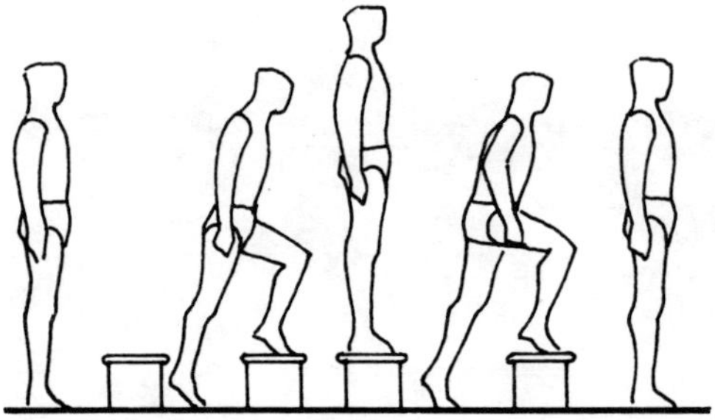

Step-ups.

Running on the spot.

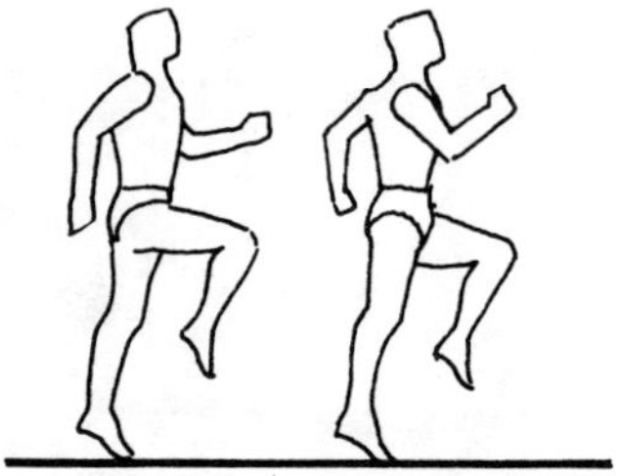

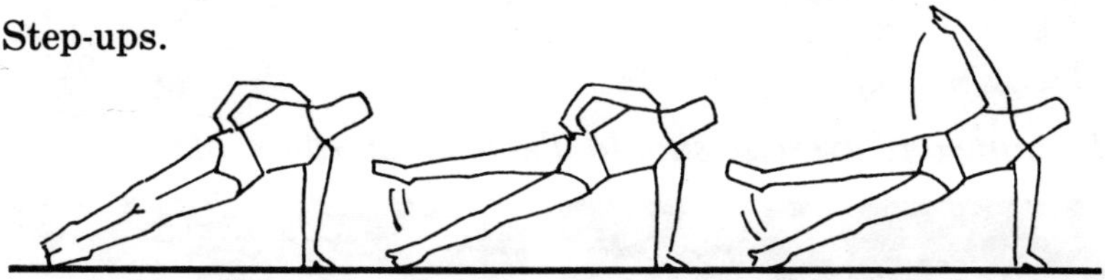

Leg signals.

Hip lift.

Two-handed tug of war.

One-handed tug of war.

Duck fighting.

Training and exercise should above all be enjoyable.

Chariots.

Neck support.

Rowing in fours.

Three against one.

Hopping push with hand on head.

Grinding Coffee — Partners face, clasp hands. Both turn completely round while maintaining the hand clasp. The movement can be continuous.

Balance Hand Wrestle — Grasp right (left) hand, raise left (right) leg. Wrestle to force partner to put foot down again. No hopping.

Sawing Logs — Partners face, one foot forward. Hands grasp with elbows high. As one arm is pulled back the other is extended well forward.

Dagger Fight — Partners pretend to strike with a dagger held in the right (left) hand. The free hand grasps the wrist of the partner's dagger hand.

Pulling and Holding Combat — Partners stand one behind other and grasp fingers. The front one aims to pull partner across a line. Partner resists.

Arm Parting — Defender raises elbows sideways so that fingertips touch across chest. Attacker grasps wrists and attempts to draw the fingers apart.

Shoulder Push — Partners face and place hands on each other's shoulders, one hand inside. The contest ends when opponent is pushed across marked line.

Chinese Get-Up — Partners sit back to back, elbows

Grinding coffee.

Sawing logs.

Balance hand wrestle.

Dagger fight.

Pulling and holding combat.

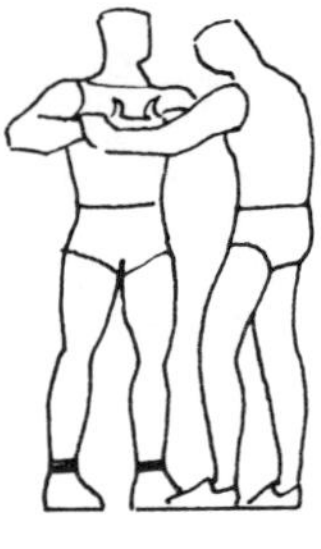

Arm parting.

Shoulder push.

linked and knees raised. Standing position is reached by extending legs.

Forearm Wrestle — Partners face, standing astride. They raise right (left) arms forward so that they cross with wrists touching. Contest is to force partner's arm across.

Elbow-Link Tug of War — Partners link right (left) elbows and pull. Extend to larger groups (four to six), facing outwards pulling, then facing inwards with arms linked. Link arms in threes. Bull in the Ring. Person in middle tries to get out.

Danish Wrestle — Partners face, grasp right (left) wrists and put right (left) foot forward so that outside border touches partners. Partners wrestle to force opponent to move his forward foot. Back foot may be moved in any direction.

Short Wheelbarrow — The 'barrow' gets down on hands with feet astride. Partner picks up the shafts above the knees and holds them firmly to his side. 'Walk' along lifting hands off ground.

Chinese get-up.

Forearm wrestle.

Elbow-link tug of war.

Danish wrestle.

Short wheelbarrow.

Groups

Select a set of six exercises to do at each training session, using either other players or whatever fixed apparatus is available. Some forward-thinking groups have erected climbing frames, chin-up bars, stools, dip bars, etc., to make a trim trail at strategic positions around their grounds. However, there are many exercises that can be done in pairs or small groups, and which can encourage competition, enthusiasm, and vigorous non-stop activity for a short period.

Rowing in Fours — Seated with finger grip and facing opposites, feet touching arms fully extended. Two opposites lean in to touch noses while others lean out. Alternate for 30 seconds.

Three against One — Three form circle with hands grasped. Player on outside trying to touch opposite. Change when touched. Vary by having one player in middle trying to break out. Use sailor grip. Change to elbow grip.

Grab the Tail — Line behind leader and hang onto the waist of the person in front. Odd man out trying to catch tail. Leader with arms outstretched.

Pendulum Carry — Arms around neck of two supports, swing legs high forwards and backwards.

Chariots — Group of four. Two front row, one lock, one free ride. Change positions after length of field.

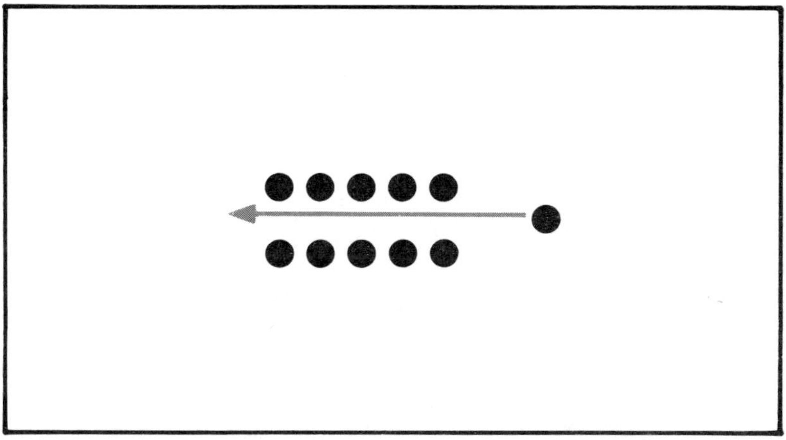

Run the Gauntlet — Group divides and players line up opposite each other, approximately one metre apart. Prisoner runs between and gets pushed from one side to the other. Open palms.

Hold the Ball — One player grasps ball firmly. On signal three others try to take ball from him. Count out loud. Allow each player a turn with the ball.

Sprint and Exercise — 10 seconds, 15 seconds, 20 seconds. All start from goal-line. On 'go' sprint non-stop except to do nominated exercise, e.g. sprint, three press-ups, one forward roll, sprint, opposite direction sprint. Perhaps use team signals, other signs or whistle to change activity.

Bump — Game of tag. All players (except two) link arms in threes. These threes stand linked in circular formation and don't move. Chaser ● tries to tag runner ○. To avoid being tagged, a runner may join onto a

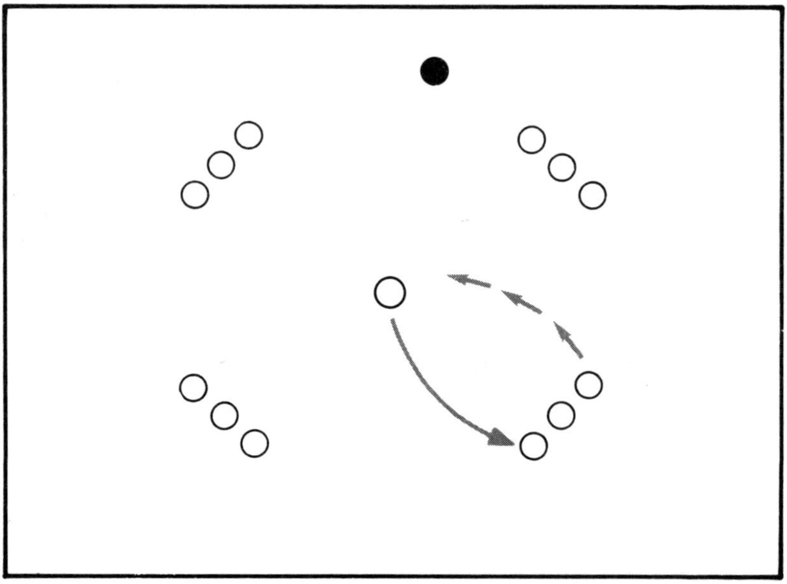

group of three. Person on other end of group is ‘bumped off’ and becomes a runner.

Pairs Tag — Players are restricted to an area about 6 × 6 metres. Two players join hands and then try to tag other players, who join the pair. When there are four in the tagged group they split into two pairs and start to build to four again — and so the process is repeated until the last person is caught.

Smuggle the Ball — Group of four to six players. One player attempts to touch ball. Other players huddle together and smuggle the ball amongst them. Players may move about but must keep in contact.

Ball Games and Relays

All players, young and old, find it easier and more fun to learn through games. Most games require very little equipment or preparation other than grid or normal ground markings. It is up to each coach to modify the size of the area, adapt the rules, and propose changes when he has evaluated the fitness, size, age and ability of his group. Here are fifty games to choose from.

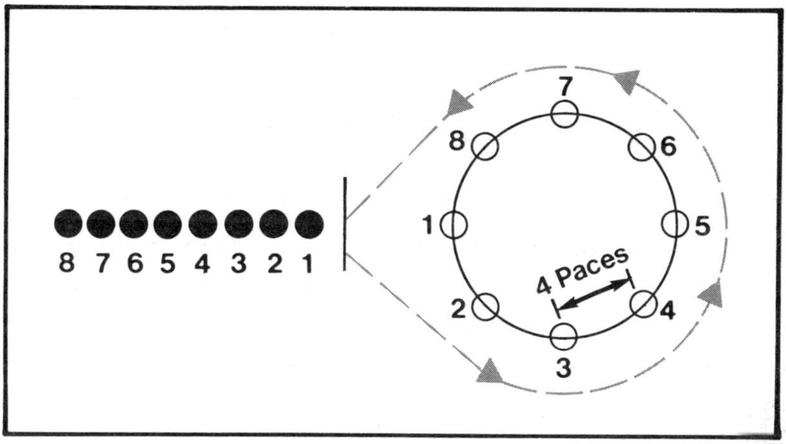

(1) Clock-Passing versus Running — The players of the first team form a circle and pass the ball as many times as possible, while the other team relay run around the outside. The first half is over when the last relay runner has completed his run. The teams then change activities. The winning team is the one with the most passes.

(2) How Many Passes — Four players in a smaller area, three against one. ● is interceptor, who tries to pressure other players into dropping or making a bad pass. If ball is intercepted or dropped, ● becomes a passer and new ● is the person who made the error.

Variations: 3 × 3, 4 × 4, 5 × 5: count how many passes are made before the ball is dropped or intercepted.

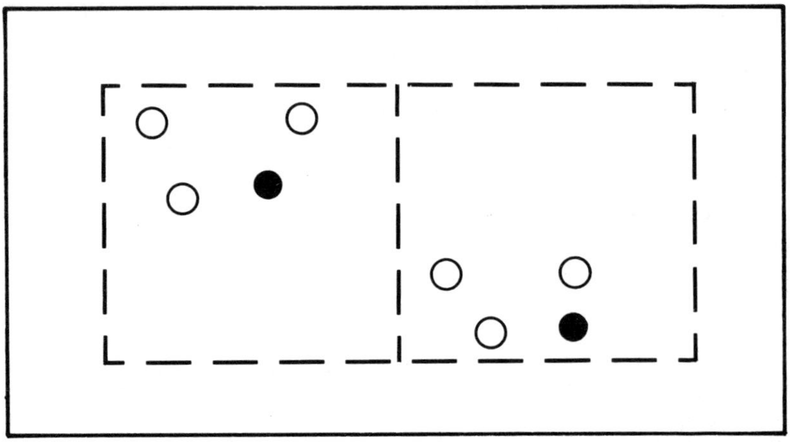

(3) Number Ball — In teams of four, five or six. Each player in the team is given a number. The ball must be passed in the order 1 — 2— 3 — 4 — 5 — 1, etc. One team begins passing in order. Players free to move around their boundary. Ball carrier cannot move once he has the ball.

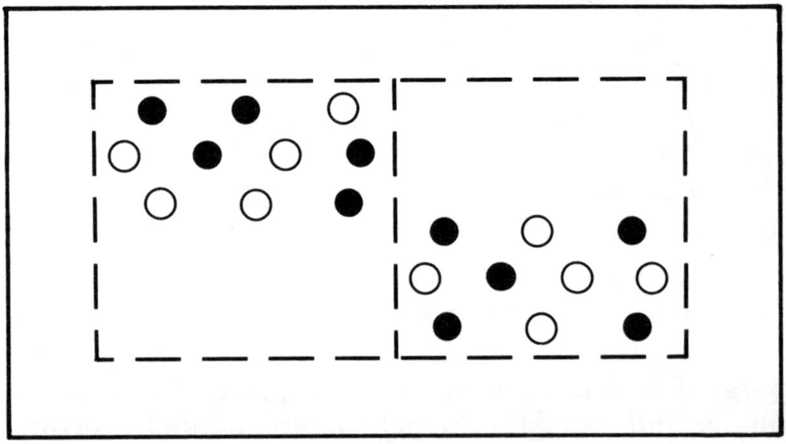

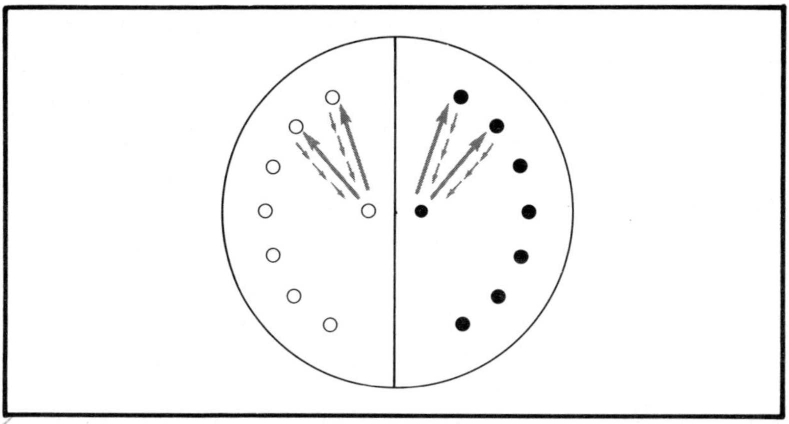

(4) Fan Formation — The game requires that the ball be passed as fast as possible. The pivot player throws the ball to each player in the fan and each throws it back. The last player to catch the ball then moves in to become the pivot, and the previous pivot goes to the top of the fan. The game ends when all players are back into their original positions. The first team to do this wins.

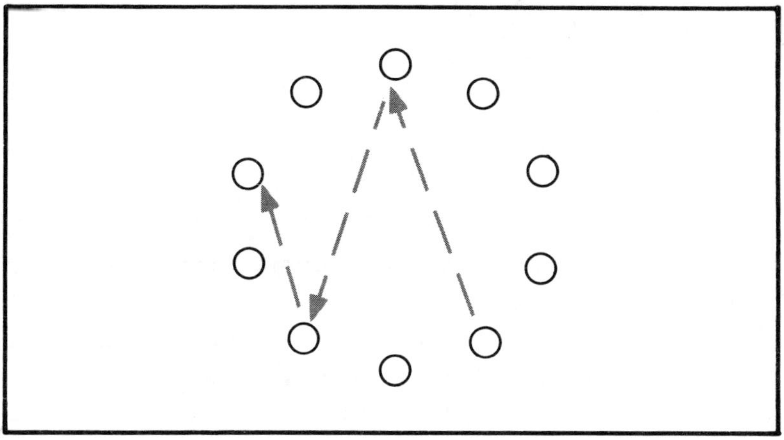

(5) Pattern Ball — Team forms a circle. The aim is to

pass the ball in the circle in an established pattern. To establish the pattern one person starts with the ball; everyone else puts one hand in the air. The starter can pass to anyone with his hand up. Once a person has received and given a pass he puts down his hand. The process is repeated until everyone has his hand down, and the ball goes back to the starter. The pattern has now been set. The ball is passed in this pattern as quickly as possible without it being dropped.

• Two, three, four, or more, balls can be introduced to keep the players alert.

• This can be varied by having the players run to where they have passed.

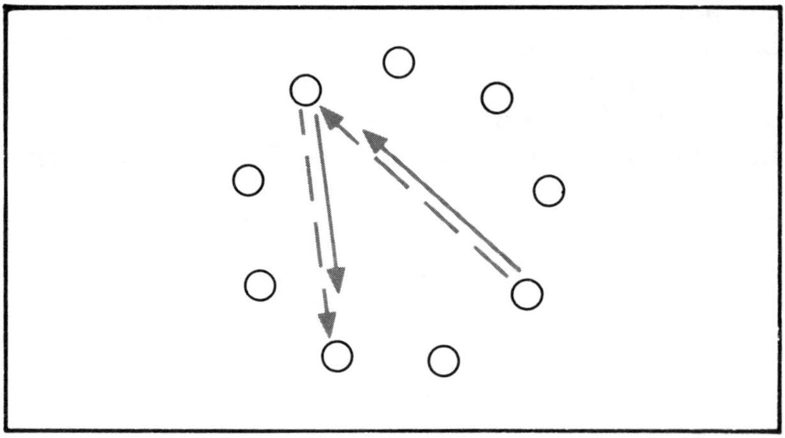

(6) Pass/Kick and Follow — Players form a circle with one ball (for a start). A pattern is set, as in Pattern Ball. The players now start to pass the ball to the same person and then follow the pass. The person you pass to will be in a different position each time.

Variations: Kick instead of pass; use different

passes; use two or more balls, depending on the level of skill of the players.

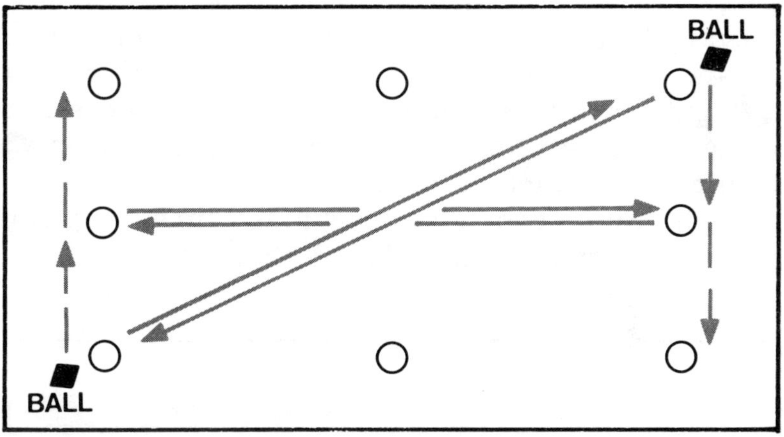

(7) Opposites — Eight players in square formation, two balls at opposite corners. Balls must be passed in the same direction. Players who have the ball pass it to the next person and then run to the position opposite.

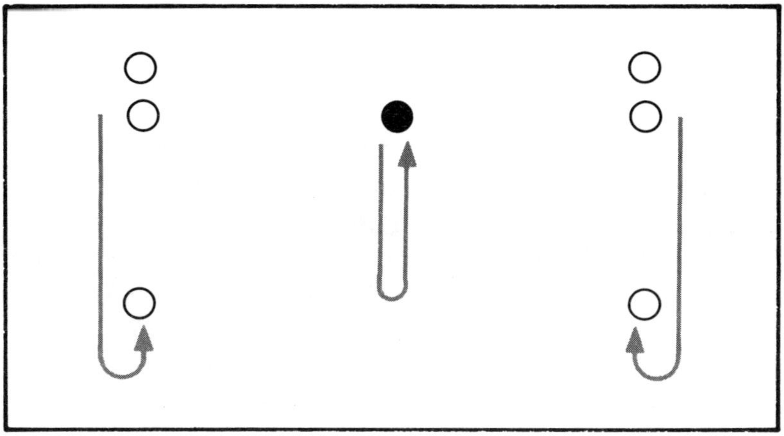

(8) Middle Run — Seven players arranged as in

diagram — distance is approximately 20-30 metres. One ball is passed along the line of ○(●)○. The ball is passed between the three as many times as possible as they run to the other end. The two outside runners drop off and the two at the other end join the middle runner (●) and go back the opposite way. This process is repeated for a set time or set number of runs — then (●) changes with another player.

Each group of three see how many times they can pass amongst themselves before they get to the other end.

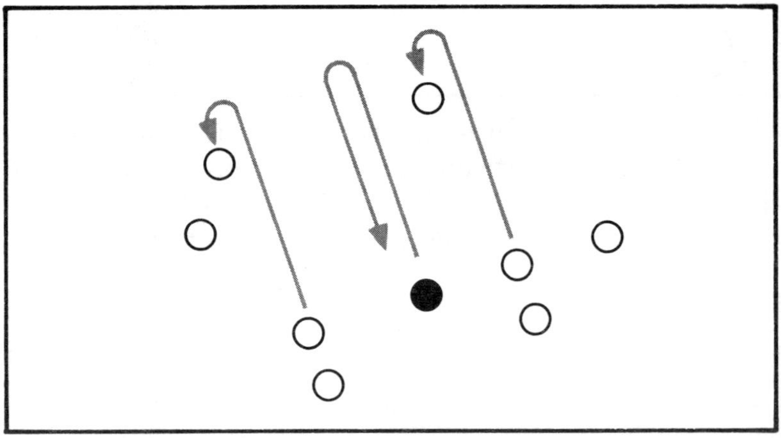

Variations: As above but with nine players, the two extras being halfbacks. The aim is to get the ball through the three before they get to the halfbacks. Halfbacks get the ball and start the other waiting backline in the opposite direction (○) turns and joins the next backline. Halfbacks begin moving closer together.

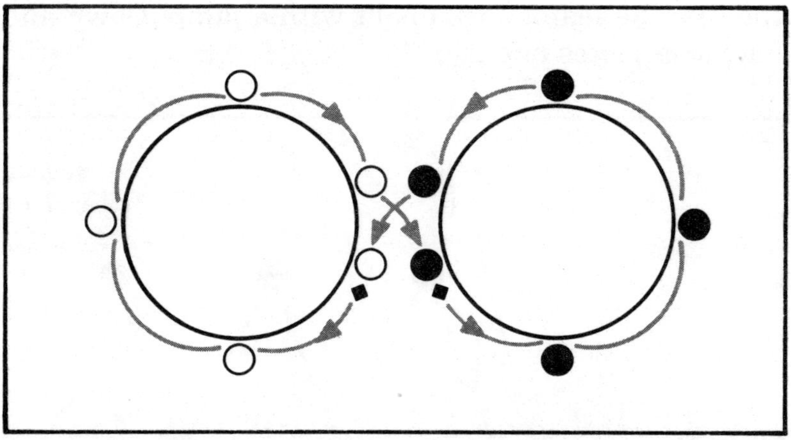

(9) Figure-Eight Passing — Two teams arranged facing outwards as shown in diagram. Two balls are passed until both are definitely in the same circle. At this stage other team scores a point and passing begins again from starting points with direction reversed. With good teams, balls may describe several figures-of-eight before they are clearly in one circle.

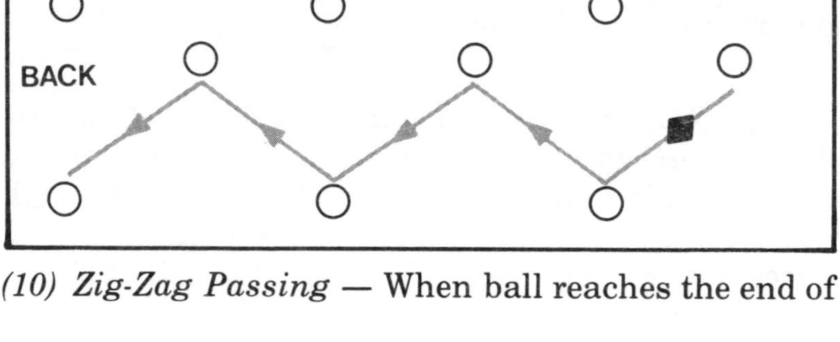

(10) Zig-Zag Passing — When ball reaches the end of

the line the teams face about with a jump. Down and back completes one trip.

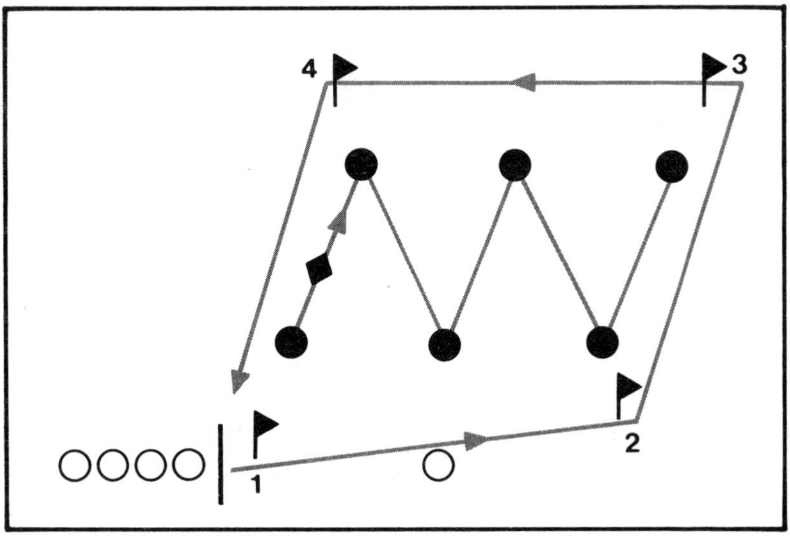

(11) Ball Pass versus Team Running — Run with ball held in two hands. In the diagram one team is passing while the other team is running (or doing one of the variations). Each team does both activities and then the passing scores are compared. Players in one team pass the ball as in Zig-Zag Passing. Other players run with the ball round the marked course, passing the ball to next runner at last mark.

(12a) Pick-up and touch-down variation — Balls are placed on ground at marks 2 and 4. First runner picks up ball at 2 and places it at 3, picks up ball at 4 and places it at 1. Second runner picks up ball at 1 and places it at 2, running on to pick up next ball at 3 and

placing at 4. Each runner starts when second ball is touched down.

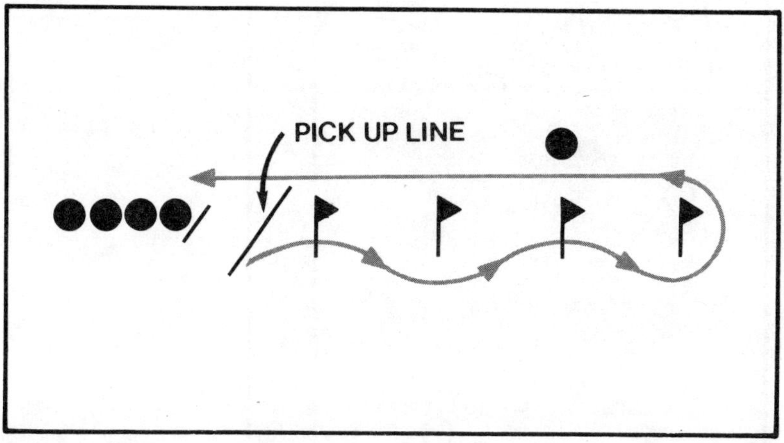

(12b) Side-step variation — Marks are arranged as in diagram in front of running team. Runner picks up ball in both hands at pick-up line, runs in and out of marks, and straight back to touch ball down. When ball is down, second runner starts.

(12c) Dribbling variation — Use last two marks of side-step formation. Runner dribbles to first mark, picks up and runs round second, and touches ball down at pick-up lines for next runner to start.

(12d) Side-step, dummy, fend, for other variations

(13) Tap and Pass — Halfback taps ball on ground. First runner runs forward at this signal to take a pass. Straightening his run, he returns pass to half and continues round to rejoin the line.

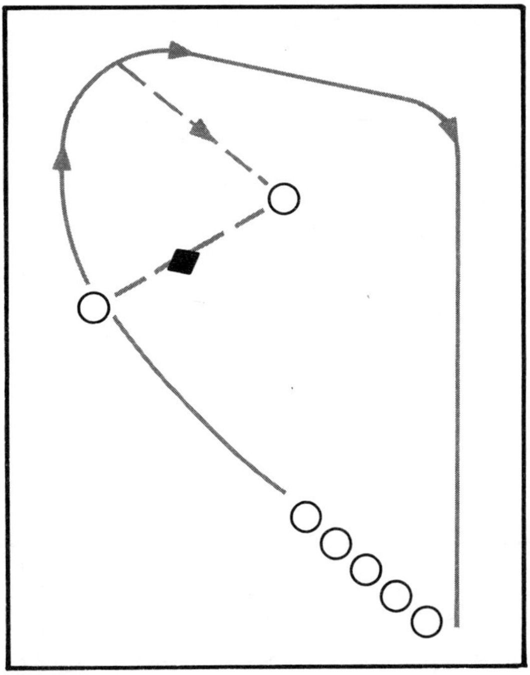

Tap and Pass

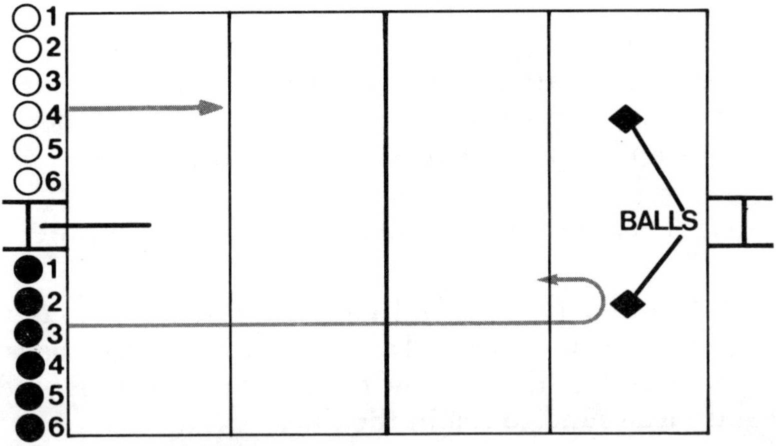

Progression Ball

(14) Progression Ball — Player O^1 runs to get the ball and tries to bring it back to his base. All ●s attempt to tackle him. The first player, O^1, remains standing at the place where he was tackled. Then ●^{1} goes for the ball, and likewise all Os attempt to tackle him. O^2 goes to release O^1 by touching him. These two try to move the ball towards the line until they are caught (no forward passes). Then ●^{2} goes for the ball. The winning team is the first to return the ball behind their own line.

(15) Piggy in the Middle — Start with as many as seven against one, seven in possession to build up rhythm and accuracy. Switch to six versus two, five versus three as standard gets better. Stress working off the ball, supporting all the time.

(16) Possession Ball (Touch Football) — Two teams of four versus four in a 20 × 22 metre area, one side in possession. The aim is to keep possession while your opponents dispute it, staying inside the area. Set targets of 10 passes, 30 seconds etc. If opposition intercept, they take over.

(17) Captain Ball — As above, but one player is made 'captain' of each team. Team in possession can only pass to captain. Set a target of five passes to captain for a score. Ball then goes to opposition.

(18) American Football (Tag) — Two sides of three versus three or four versus four inside 22 m line, playing across the field. Scoring by touch-down over the sideline between the 22 m line and goal-line. Passing can be forward, backwards or sideways. When tagged, player in possession must stand still.

Opposition gets the ball if it spills to ground or is intercepted.

(19) Target Man (Tag) — As above, but instead of try-scoring, the ball must be passed to a target man, who is put behind the opposing team's defending goal-line and not allowed into the field of play. The ball must be cleanly caught for a score, and target men changed frequently.

(20) Touch Football — As above, but with try-scoring over the side-lines and the restriction on the forward pass.

(21) Ball versus Runner — Team in a circle; distance to be determined by throw used. Runner No. 1 starts with the ball, passes to right or left, then leaves place in the circle, running around circle in same direction as ball passed. Meanwhile, the rest of team pass ball right around circle until it arrives at the person who first received it from the runner. If the runner arrives in his position to receive the ball, he gains a point. Immediately the person who first had the ball passed to him receives it after the runner has completed the circle, he then becomes the runner, and so on. Thus each runner is competing in turn against the team.

If first pass is dropped, runner must start again (this runner must not give a poor pass). Each player in circle must receive a pass. The player who drops the ball must retrieve it.

(22) Ball Chase Around Circle — Players form circle (spaced according to throw or pass). Two or more balls spaced evenly around circle. Players pass ball around circle trying to overtake ball in front. Insist on

specified throw or pass.

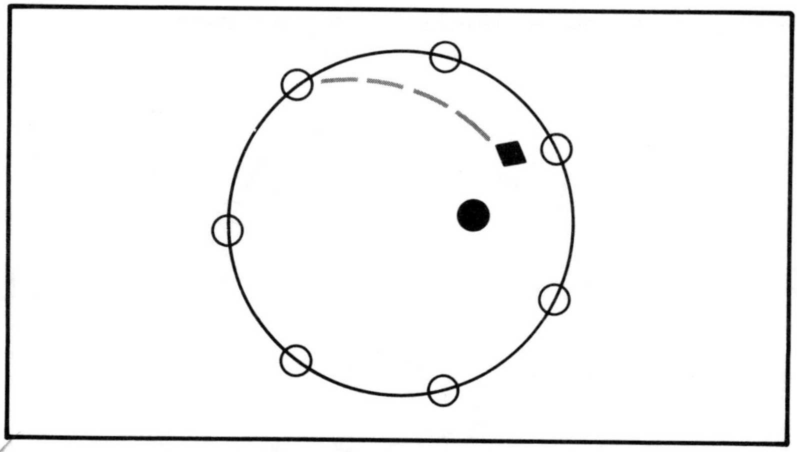

(23) Wandering Ball — For drawing the opposition, widening vision, feinting, team work and fast passing.

Players form a circle. The ball is passed from player to player no higher than the full reach of the interceptor, who attempts to touch the ball or a player in possession. The ball cannot be thrown to the player on either side of the passer. The interceptor cannot leave the circle. If the interceptor stops or touches a held ball or any part of the player holding the ball, he replaces the player who last played the ball or the player who was touched.

Teaching points:

- Draw the interceptor before passing the ball.
- The interceptor should continually move to intercept the ball or touch the ball holder.
- When the ball handling is of a high standard, increase the difficulty for the passers by introducing a second interceptor.

• Two interceptors: the players should draw one and pass to a gap left by the second.
• The interceptors should develop teamwork.

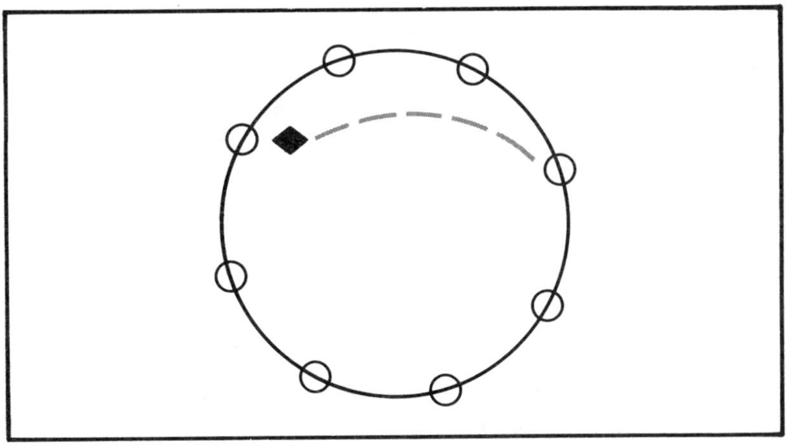

(24) Keep the ball moving — For maintaining balanced body position square-on to ball, fluid catch-throw, passing from where you catch, and backing up.

Players form a circle and pass the ball across the circle as often as possible in 30 seconds. The ball cannot be thrown to the two players on either side of the thrower. Try to better own team's score and/or that of the opposing team.

Variation: Pass then run to take place of person to whom you have passed.

(25) Team Dodge Ball — Large ball. Up to 12 players. Defending players in a file using waist grip.

Attacking players try to hit last player in the file below the waist. Dodgers may move to prevent this, provided they maintain hold. End player joins attackers when file is broken or if hit. The game continues until the last dodger has been hit. Change

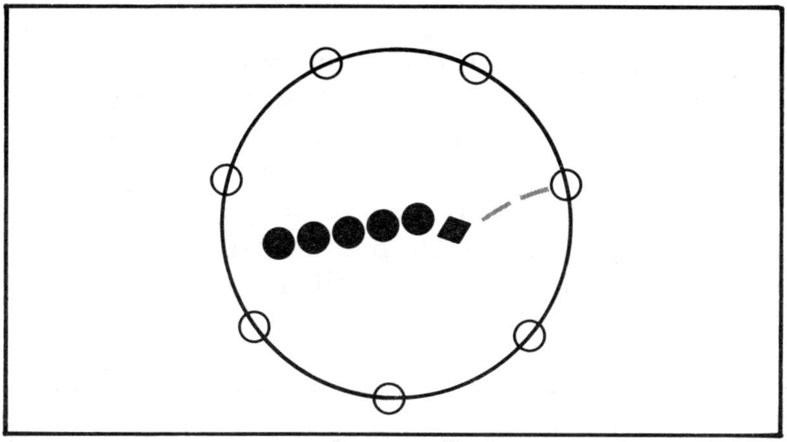

over. Attackers should be encouraged to pass to each other before trying to hit the dodgers.

Variations: Divide dodgers into two teams; game may be played to a time limit, counting successful hits.

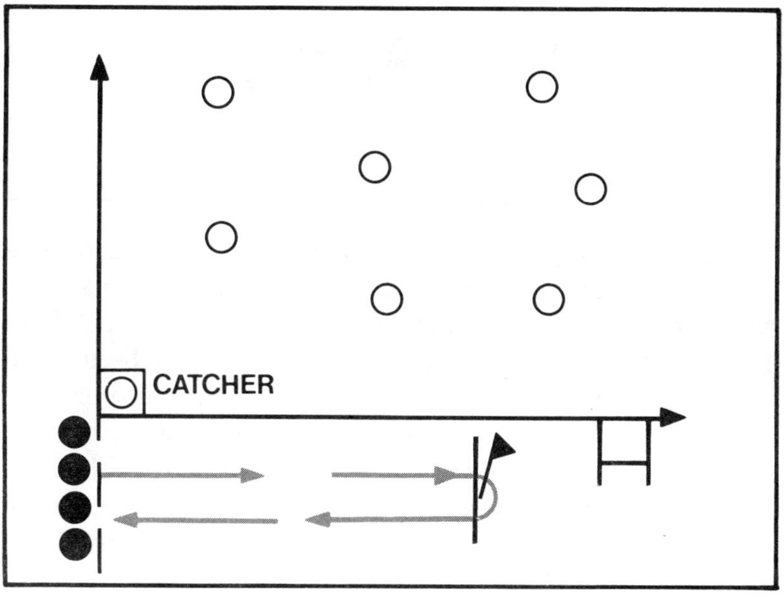

Scatter Ball (see over)

(26) Scatter Ball — Three balls in softball area. Players (in turn) in the kicking team kick the three balls forward within lines. Any ball foul of this area is disqualified. Player scores a point for each time he makes a complete run out around mark and back. Fielders return balls by kicking them back to catcher, or via other fieldsmen. Dropped ball must be retrieved by another fielder. Catcher calls stop when last ball has been returned to home base.

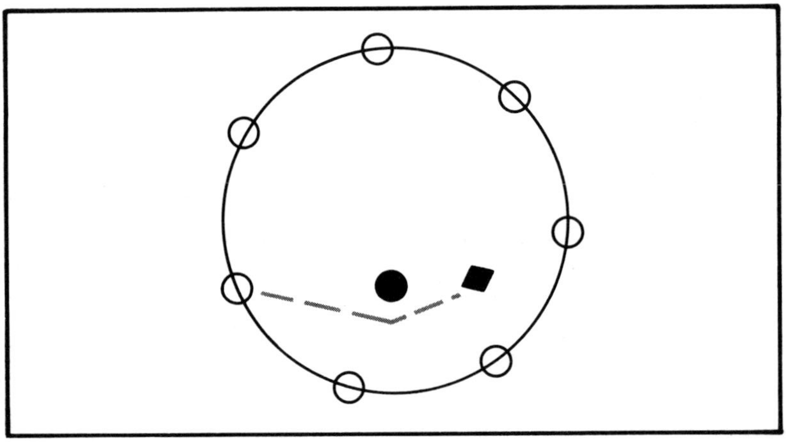

(27) Circle Dodge — Large ball. Players form circle as in diagram. Aim is to hit the dodger below the knees. All throws must be made from outside the circle. The dodger may use his hands to protect his legs. The successful thrower becomes the dodger. A player who has already been a dodger may choose another to take his place. If a player enters the circle to retrieve the ball he must give it to a player outside. Attackers should be encouraged to pass to each other before trying to hit the dodger.

Grid Training

The Coaching Grid

The use of a coaching grid for team sports has been widely accepted for many years. Although rugby coaches have often unwittingly utilised the first principle of a coaching grid — that of restricting the working area — the system has never been properly developed.

A grid is a series of 10-metre squares marked out on a convenient part of a field. A rugby field, already divided by many lines, lends itself to a quick conversion into grids using cone markers, as shown in the diagram.

There is no doubt that the coaching grid is of great benefit for acquiring skills and accelerating the learning process. In a restricted area coaches can intensify the work rate and exercise tighter control over the group.

Once the idea of many separate small playing areas is accepted, it is up to the coach to decide how to use the grids. It is essential that the drills used are practical and well devised. If not, senior players will tend to treat the training as child's play, where in fact it can be highly productive and physically demanding. Players can also be encouraged to work out their own drills to add to the variety.

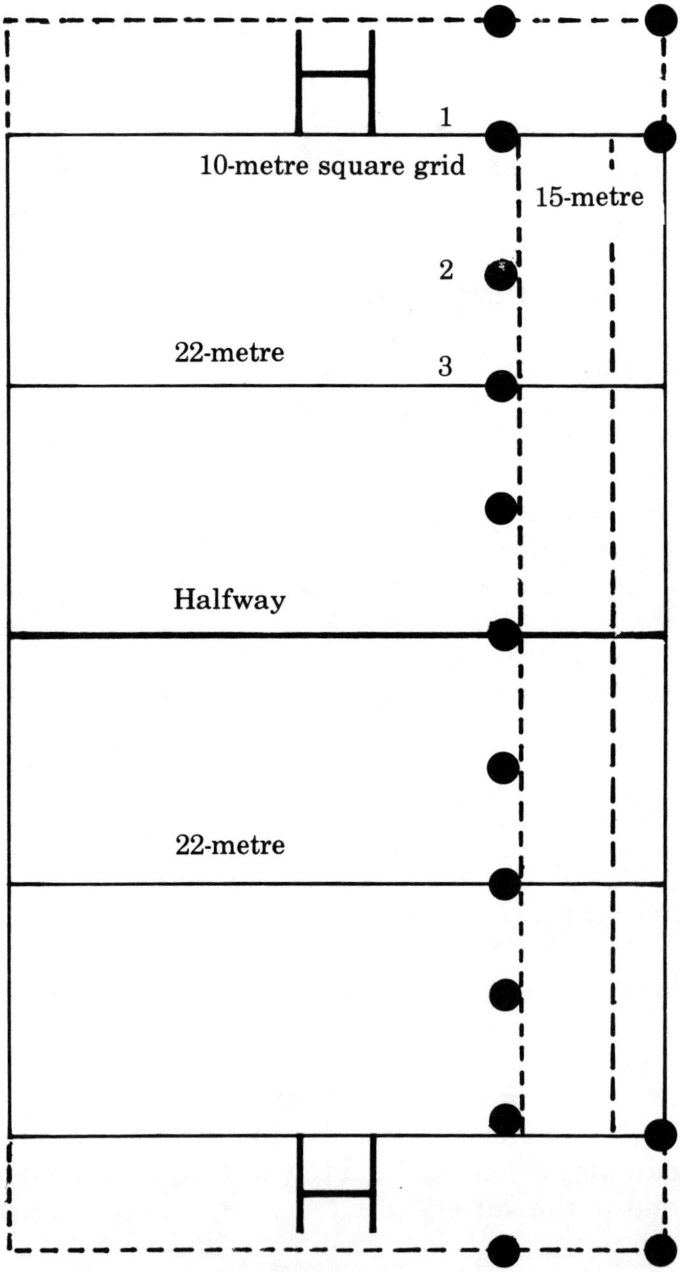
1
10-metre square grid
15-metre
2
22-metre
3
Halfway
22-metre

(A) PASSING • Low pass • Miss pass • High pass • Flick pass	(B) SCRUMMAGING • Body position • In pairs/threes • Tight five
(H) TACKLING • Pairs • Tractor tube • Tackle bags	(C) RUNNING • Short sprints • Side-stepping • Change of pace
(G) LINEOUT • Touch crossbar • Jump and take • Deflecting	(D) CATCHING • High ball • Low ball • Rolling ball
(F) MAUL • 3 v 1 • 4 v 4	(E) KICKING • In pairs • Grubber • Punt

The coaching grid imposed on a rugby field.

Grid Activity

Using Small Areas — Six grids are used for improving the passing of a group. Each grid could contain three or four players, depending on the activity chosen. In this case, three are put into each grid, B and C playing against A. The objective of B and C is to cross the opposite boundary line of the grid without being touched. If touched, they start again. Best of five attempts within the group. Combine Grid 1 with Grid 2, and so on, and have four versus two or, as they develop further skills, have three versus three or six versus six, etc.

This progression would not necessarily be achieved in one lesson. At a later stage, when reverse pass, skip pass, tackling and other forms of elusiveness have been taught, the initial two versus one game could be reintroduced with the new skills.

Using the Whole Field — Some teaching points:

Passing — (a) Walking pace, (b) Running, (c) Have depth and run onto ball.

Scrummaging — (a) Feet position, (b) Lower hips, (c) Raise eyebrows.

Running — (a) Ball held in two hands, (b) Fending/-dodging markers, (c) General elusiveness.

Catching — (a) Kicking or throwing to nominated player, (b) Turn body for high ball, (c) Back up the catcher, work in threes or pairs.

Kicking — (a) In pairs. Direction rather than length, (b) Both feet.

Aim to train hard and with purpose.

Maul — (a) Standing tackles, (b) Lower body and spread feet, (c) Twist body.

Lineout — (a) Straight feed/drive, (b) Thrower-jumper-half back. Work in threes, (c) Deflection/take.

Tackling — (a) In pairs, (b) Body position, (c) Drive off one foot, aim for a point beyond.

Simple Routine — Could be used for beginners as well as seniors. Apart from showing the value of grids, this session will also highlight some of the teaching points.
(1) In groups of three, let players run across the field and back.
(2) Reduce the area to, say, within the goal-line and 22 m line and up to the goalpost, and have all the groups of three passing and moving around at random. Teach aim of pass, speed of pass, and type of pass.

(3) Let them do the same thing at greater speed. This will tend to create more mistakes, as players are now under pressure. Encourage them to move around a lot more. Vary the pass, and work the ball a lot harder. Use the whole area, looking for space.
(4) Reduce size of grid to 10-metre square with, say, three groups of three per grid. Players still pass to one another within their original group. Use the whole area to move around. Vary pass according to whether the receiver is moving away from or towards the passer. Watch where you are passing the ball. Avoid allowing a player from another group to get in the way.
(5) Change back to three per grid and introduce some pressure by counting the number of passes in 20 seconds. Introduce an interceptor, (two versus one).
(6) More physical contact can be introduced in the form of mauling for the ball and standing tackles, still working three per grid.
(7) As the skills develop, pressure can be increased to a three versus two or four versus two contest. Change about as ball is dropped or intercepted. Promote a competitive atmosphere.
(8) The competition can be expanded as the skills improve: three versus three to commence; increase grid size for six versus six; eight versus eight competing in ball games; backs versus forwards, or odds versus evens.

You will find, as will the players, that this form of training increases fitness, and ball handling will show a marked improvement. There are many routines on a particular theme that can be planned to suit the needs of your players. Participation through grid sessions encourages competitiveness and helps develop team spirit because all are actively involved in the training session.

Teaching and Coaching

Coaching begins after teaching has taken place. Even at international level, the players are still learning. The coach is mainly concerned with organising, motivating and polishing, some teaching is involved. The main functions of the coach should be to teach players individual and group skill in order to give them sufficient options to help produce a higher standard of achievement.

Perfect practice makes perfect.

Unit Training: The Forward Unit

Mastering and Developing the Skills

A high level of confidence and competence in **scrummaging** can be achieved only by mastering the skills of body positions, feet positions, gripping procedures and timing, all through hard, repetitive training. There is no easy way of achieving high levels of performance otherwise. It requires total commitment to hours of practice.

Secondly, it has to be understood by coaches and teams just how much influence **lineouts** have on the course of a game. There has been some despair about our lineout game in New Zealand since the major changes in the rules, particularly those related to spacing. I find many coaches more frustrated by the inability of the team to develop sound lineout play than by any other aspect of play. Again it is only by a full commitment to repetitive drills, including positioning, timing, support play, ball maintenance and distribution, that progress will be made. But the important point is that there can be progress, despite the current lineout laws.

The third objective is to win the battle for **second-phase possession.** It has to be clearly understood that the strike force has to be at the scene first. No amount of skill and commitment at the ruck or maul will compensate for being beaten to the break-downs by the opposition, or even by one member of the opposition if their support play is good. This is why the fast, pressurising, ball-hungry open-side flanker (or lineout No. 8) with ball-handling skills is so dominant in modern rugby. No team can afford to be without such a player. The role of backs at the break-down should not be forgotten — if they are the nearest to the ball, it's their job to go in after it and get it.

Good possession for you or bad possession for the opposition during a scrum will result from forward momentum imparted by low body positioning and driving. It is surprising how many of a team's other inadequacies can be compensated for by the total commitment of eight forwards to hitting the break-downs hard and low and keeping on hitting.

The major role of the forwards is to win the ball. Specialists have their particular roles, but in the main this unit must support the ball and work together forcefully.

There are certain tasks that the forwards perform as a unit. These are the scrum, the line-out, the ruck and the maul.

The Scrum

A total of about 50 scrums will occur in the average 80-minutes rugby match. A good scrummage is the basis of a good team. It is of vital importance because:

- On your ball you aim for quality ball — you have an advantage on your put-in to the scrum

- You have positive options to exercise
- You can develop set drills
- On opposition ball a good scrum means an opportunity to apply pressure, not only to the opposition pack, but also to their backs.

Every member of the unit must take a full part in the exercise. The 'hard core' of the scrummage consists of the 'tight five': hooker, two props and two locks. A strong scrum is achieved by constant practice and application of the correct techniques. A small scrum that is technically sound can outplay a larger pack that has no method or technique. Once sound scrummaging techniques have been established, the benefits will be quickly seen in the rucking and mauling performances of the team.

Basic Body Position — Have two players go down in a pushing position and observe the following points:

Back and neck — Power is transmitted through the spine and shoulders, and is greatest if the back is made rigid and the back and neck are both straight. The head must also be forced up — hence the common saying 'heads up — raise the eyebrows'.

Legs — It is important to have both feet back and

shoulder-width apart to get the explosive push.

Hips and knees — On a given signal hips sink to a position below the shoulder. Knees bent for leverage are straightened, and with forward pressure we achieve a powerful result.
'Squeeze . . . si . . . ink, Weight!'

With knees slightly bent we have a pushing position and with knees straight we have a locking position. The effect gained by the pusher straightening his knees while aiming his body down and forward with a thrust is convincing and leaves no doubt as to the correct technique to adopt and develop.

Forming the scrum

Hooker

- Hooker's arms are placed over props' arms.
- Hooker grips props under outside armpits.
- All grips should be tight and unable to be broken by a sudden pull.
- All players should be as comfortable as possible.

Props — To obtain a correct grip the props start behind the hooker and grasp his jersey, not his shorts, in the vicinity of the hooker's navel. While maintaining this grip, the props walk round the hooker into their correct positions. The loose-head is first on the ball. If the grip is correct, the props, by the extension of their arms, should lift the hooker clear of the ground.

Note in the photographs on the following page:

- Props have gripped the jersey of the hooker close to his mid-line and have walked round into their positions.

- The hooker is gripping the props' jerseys under the armpits.
- All three players are tightly bound together.
- Props must wrench their inside shoulder forward to present a flat-fronted scrum.

Forming the scrum: Prop grips hooker's jersey and walks round alongside him.

Make sure that the props have reached far enough round the hooker in taking their initial grip, and there are no gaps where props' and hooker's shoulders meet and there is little likelihood of the opposition being able to create one.

Setting the front row — Start by establishing grips as outlined and by having shoulders, hips and feet square and parallel to the goal-line. The feet should be spaced at least as wide apart as the shoulder width of the prop, with the knees slightly bent. Allow sufficient distance from opponents to take a normal pace towards them with outside feet of both the loose- and tight-head props. At the same time retain weight on inside feet, which should not move at all.

Having stepped up with outside feet and made contact with the opposing front row, return players to their former positions. The loose-head prop may have his left foot about 25 cm in advance of his right. The pace up is to lower the body position for contact.

Make sure that the props' feet are apart to provide both space for the hooked ball and stability, and that any forward movement of the scrum, after it is set to go down, does not upset its stability.

Ensure that:

- Props have straight backs and heads back.
- Loose-head prop's left foot in advance of the right.
- Loose-head prop's left hand gripping opponent in the small of the back.
- Tight-head prop's feet apart and back (not directly under hips).
- The tight binding of all players.

Locks — Each lock reaches round his partner with the inside hand and inserts his thumb inside the top of his partner's shorts in the 'fob pocket' position, and grasping the outside of the shorts with his remaining fingers. Once this grip has been achieved, an outward rotation of the wrist will ensure that the inside thighs of the locks are tightly drawn together. This grip must be retained for the duration of the scrum.

The outside hand goes round the outside leg of the prop and secures a firm grip on the front of the thigh. By retaining this grip and turning the wrist over, the elbow is raised to allow the flanker to pack his shoulder under the rump of the prop.

Locks hook their thumbs into the top of their partner's shorts and grasp the outside of the shorts with the remaining fingers.

- Make sure that the locks' grips are firm and unable to be broken by pulling.
- Encourage the locks to pull with the hand that binds them together.
- The locks should rotate wrists outward to facilitate close binding at thigh level.
- Ensure that the lock's outside hand and arm are not obstructing the flanker.

Note the variation in this photograph:

- Locks have placed their arms between the props' legs.
- The grip has been taken on the waistband and jersey of the prop.

- The outside hips of the props are unobstructed, making it easier for the flanker to pack.
- The lock who is gripping between the props' legs does not restrict the props' range of movement.
- The lock's grip on the prop is firm and unable to be broken by pulling.
- Remember to push fist of hand holding props' jersey inwards; do not pull down on jersey.

To achieve good feet and body positions, both locks kneel on their outside knees directly behind the front row, keeping ankles, calves, and thighs of inside legs pressed hard together as if in a three-legged race. As props take their pace forward, the locks extend their legs are far as possible backwards, while still retaining the bent-knee position. Both inside feet in the final pushing position should be about one boot length in front of the outside feet.

Ensure that the locks are comfortable, that they flatten their backs and keep their heads back, and that their inside feet are slightly forward.

Flankers — The flankers grasp the locks' jerseys in the middle of the back, extending right or left arm.

Each flanker places his inside foot alongside the outside foot of the prop, thereby bringing his shoulder under the rump of the prop. He then brings his inside foot back to full extent and slightly forward of the outside foot.

It is important that:

- The flankers pack under the rumps of the props.
- The whole scrum is completely packed before the front row attempts to go down.
- Flankers play a full part in achieving a solid well-

packed scrummage.

In this practice scrum the front rows are too high, the result of being too close to each other when they went down.

No. 8 — The back-row man grips each lock on his outside hip. He keeps his head back and pushes his head between the hips of the locks. His shoulders make contact below the curve of the rump, and his legs are extended to the maximum but still retain a bent-knee position.

Ensure that:

- No. 8 has his shoulders under the rumps of the locks and is able to exert maximum pressure.
- All legs in a scrummage are bent to allow maximum effort on the thrust.
- No. 8's first duty is to apply weight in scrummage until the ball is clear.

The thrust

If scrummaging is to be effective, the weight must be applied at the right time and in the right direction. To achieve this all members of the unit must be in the correct positions, and the seven forwards supporting the hooker must concentrate on delivering the thrust at the appropriate time.

Note that:

- The thrust produced by the back five is directed through the props, giving the hooker as much freedom as possible.
- Flankers must push hard to compensate for the weight coming from the locks and No. 8.
- The flankers' weight is essential to the solidity of the scrum; without it, the props can quite easily be split away.
- Make sure that the weight is transmitted through the props to give the hooker maximum mobility.

The thrust forward, which allows the hooker to operate, must be synchronised with the halfback

Side view of thrust. Line of thrust is low, hard and up under the opposing scrum.

putting in the ball. Select a signal for the team. The halfback must ensure that the scrummage is steady and that the ball can be seen by all its members. At the appropriate time the scrummage should lower slightly and, as the ball enters, thrust *forward* and *upward.*

Any lowering of the scrum, once it has been set, should be controlled by the players gently pushing their knees towards the ground. This ensures that the position with heads back and backs straight will be maintained.

Practice scrum demonstrating thrust against scrum machine.

- Co-ordinate the effort of the thrust.
- Make the halfback aware of his responsibilities.
- Ensure that any lowering of the scrum is initiated by the knees of the forwards.
- Check any lowering movement which disintegrates the scrummage.
- Have halfback or loose-head flanker call initial commands:

'Squeeze' — Grips tighten.
'Steady' — Lock scrum — slight straightening of knees — more weight on shoulders.
'Sink' — Push knees forward and lower hips.
'Weight' — All call as ball is put in.

Note that:

- All knees have been straightened.
- Thrust has been directed *forward* and *upward.*

It is important that all forwards sustain the forward thrust until the ball is clear.

Ball control

Scrummage responsibilities do not end as soon as the ball has been hooked. If the backs are to be given suitable ball to use, the ball must be controlled while forward momentum is maintained.

Note that:

- Channel (A) directs the ball between the loose-head prop's feet and through the broad passage between the flanker and the locks. The halfback receives the ball quickly, but he is vulnerable to the attentions of the opposition halfback and flanker.
- Channel (B) shows the ball being directed between the lock's feet and across to the right-hand side of the

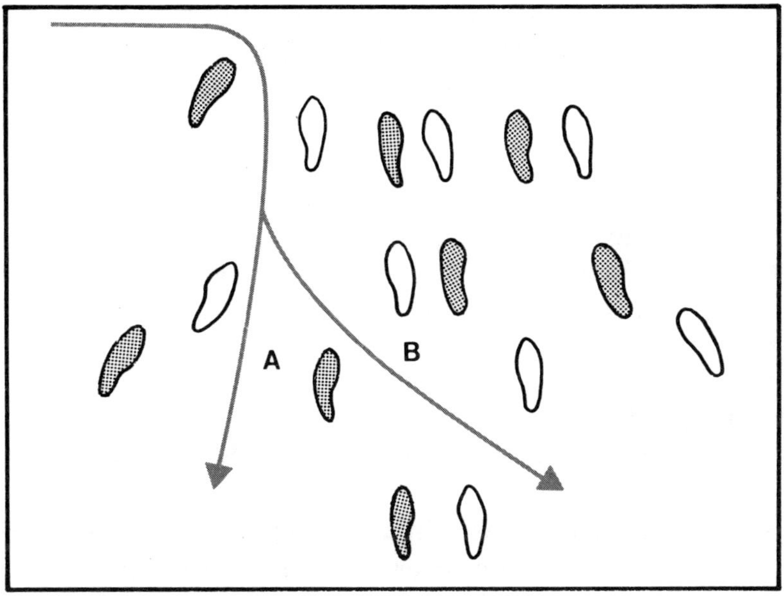

Channels for the ball.

No. 8. Once the ball rests in this position the halfback is free from the attentions of the opposition halfback and flanker and is able to play the ball unobstructed.

Make sure that the loose-head flanker is aware of his responsibility to direct the ball across between the locks' legs when using Channel B, and the No. 8 is able to control the ball until the halfback asks for it.

Hooking — The hooker is the key man in the scrum.

Under the laws he is permitted to hook with either foot and should practise on each side with each foot. The ball may be hooked once it has entered the scrum and touched the ground on the midline past the inside shoulder of the loose-head prop. The halfback and hooker must co-ordinate the put-in and the strike.

As the strike is made, the hooker extends his leg from the knee, making contact with the ball at the landing point. For the sake of speed he should move his foot in a straight line to the landing point. If the strike is timed correctly, the ball will shoot back through the channel made by the props' feet.

Ensure that:

- The halfback and front row have the opportunity to practise at each training session, so that their timing becomes perfect.
- The halfback is not putting the ball too far into the scrum.
- The hooker is striking straight for the landing point and not swinging.
- The loose-head prop's feet are so placed that the ball moves between them after having been hooked.

The position of the No. 8 — Taking the No. 8 out of the ideal pushing position — with his head between the two locks — is not encouraged. Between the loose-head lock and the loose-head flanker, the No. 8 does not push effectively and is not capable of maintaining a tight grip on the locks' bottoms to keep them in place. But occasionally, if the hooker is very quick, or if a player of the calibre of the 1970s All Black Sid Going, is the defensive halfback, or if the scrum is right on top, you may have to put the No. 8 into that area to control the hook.

When the ball is lost — When we lose the ball from a scrum the first job of the flankers is to make sure the halfback doesn't run. Some coaches do allow the halfback on one side of the scrum to take the place of the flanker, and thus release the flanker to go straight to play. It is also the flankers' responsibility to make sure that any ploys around the scrum by the opposing No. 8 or by the loose forwards in conjunction with the halfback are stopped before they reach the advantage line. For that reason I think it is simpler and clearer for defensive loose forwards not to move into the open field until the ball is away from the scrum.

To return to the No. 8. We have lost the scrum ball and the ball is now passed. The first objective has been achieved: the flankers have forced the ball to be passed to the first five-eighth or to a back. At this point, if the play has gone open side, the open-side flanker again

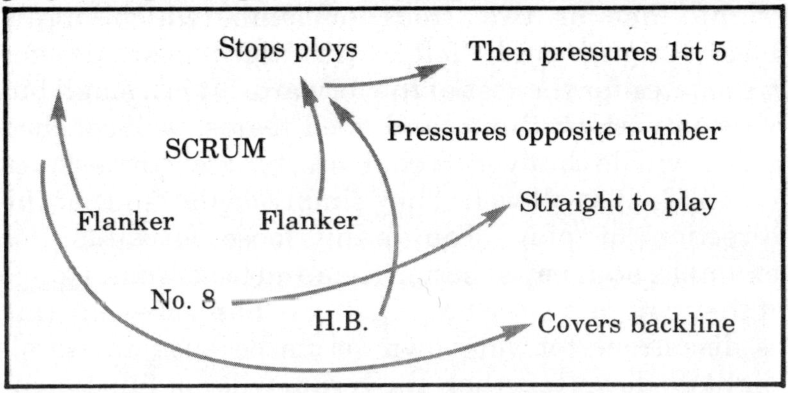

Defence when ball is lost and opposition sending it along their backline.

provides cover defence. If a loose forward is running deep — and he will do so only if the ball has got out to the outside backs — then it is the blind-side flanker's job to provide the cover, not the No. 8's. I believe there are two offensive-defensive forwards from a scrum on a lost ball: open-side flanker and No. 8. The defensive player who gives depth is the blind-side flanker.

Communicating verbally — It is essential that the

players — the loose forwards, in particular — know in which direction the play is heading. Every time the ball is put into a scrum by a halfback a clear sign is needed to indicate the direction of the ball.

Our key man in the scrum, when the ball is being put in by the opposition, is our tight-head flanker, because he sees the halfback — he is right beside him — and he calls the play for the rest of the scrum. He watches the opposing halfback's hands, and when the hands move and the ball is about to come in our tight-head flanker calls 'weight'. He should also listen very carefully for the opposition's signals. If their signals are 'left' or 'right', 'one' or 'two', 'rock' or 'lamb' (which simply mean 'right' and 'left'), the tight-head flanker translates for the rest of the forwards. It is a small but very important thing, and good teams, well-coached sides, will do that very well. Unfortunately, most sides do not do it at all well. They simply do not find out the direction of play. Too many loose forwards, for example, stand up at scrum time and look around to see if they can find out what is going to happen — and this is disastrous for your own scrum because unless all eight go down together, the scrum will not function at all.

When the ball goes to the blind side — We will now deal with attacking and defensive positions of loose forwards on the blind side. Obviously the halfback's most effective supporting forward must initially be the No. 8, because as soon as the halfback moves right or left, the No. 8 is immediately on-side. The blind-side flanker is still ahead of play until play reaches him, so the most effective supporting forward on attack on the

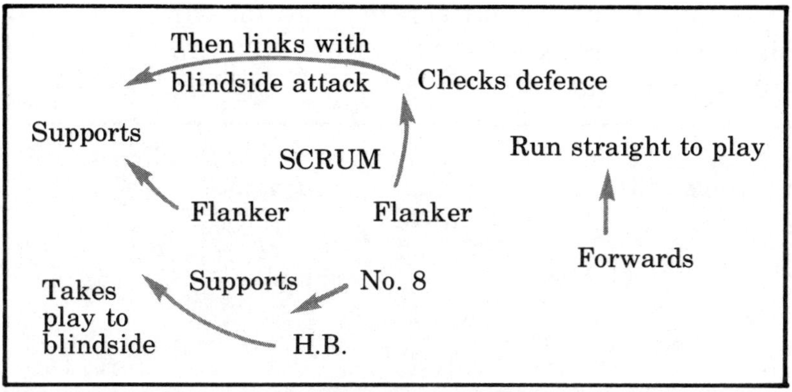

Attack when ball is won and going blindside.

blind side must be the No. 8, who therefore becomes a very critical player.

A competent open-side flanker, when the play is on the blind side, can become the next most effective supporting player. He knows it is going blind, he has a good ear, and he knows we are running away from him and he can leave the scrum quickly to support a blind-side move.

With the knowledge that the ball is coming back into play during a blind-side move, the rest of the forwards run straight to play towards the touch line, not worrying about a centre-kick.

If the ball reaches the winger and he centre-kicks, one of the backs is responsible. It is not fair to ask a loose or any other forward to try to anticipate a centre-kick from the blind side or, for that matter, from the open side. Rugby is a game of percentages, and the centre-kick percentage is very low.

What defence can we offer against the opposition running on the blind side? If there is a wide blind on defence — a very dangerous situation for any scrum —

it is important for our scrum to go forward. The first defensive strategy is to scrum well and give the opposition bad ball.

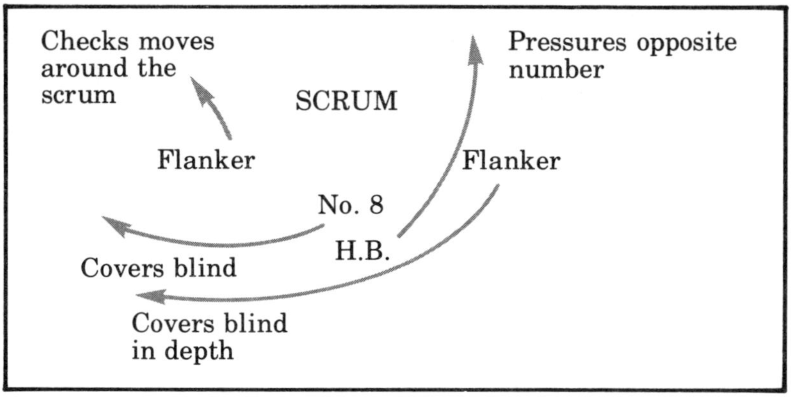

Defence against a blindside attack.

This means that everybody pushes, including our hooker. After we've pushed them back, or made it difficult for them to win the ball, the first forward to leave the scrum when there is a wide blind side must be the No. 8. When a ball is lost, the No. 8 stands up and looks to see if play is going to the blind side. In fact, some coaches have trained the No. 8 to automatically move blind side first when there is a wide blind. This means that the lost effective defensive forward is on the blind side early. It is logical to run the backs to the wide blind side. You can insist that the No. 8 gets off and moves blind. He is your best offensive-defensive forward on a wide blind when you have lost the ball. The other two flankers also have a set job: to see that no one moves around the scrum. The halfback doesn't run blind; if he does run, he is chopped. He cannot be allowed to set up a move like the Canterbury/Alex

Wyllie move with any loose forward around him on the blind side. If he does, it is the blind-side flanker's job to nail one man — if he puts one out of play, he has fulfilled his role. His main task is to allow no one on his side to cross the advantage line. The open-side flanker covers the back of the scrum on to the blind side, with the third loose forward as in-depth cover.

Defence from the scrum against a kick — To defend against good kicking from the scrum is much more difficult. For instance, some backs use the grubber kick very well. I would use a No. 8 in this situation. If we have lost the ball and there is a player who chips a lot — 1983 All Black Wayne Smith is a good kicker, open and blind — I believe it's the No. 8 who has to deal with such a defensive situation. He has the time and is in deep enough at the base of the scrum when the ball is lost to move out into the field quickly. The No. 8 then becomes the key defensive loose forward if you are up against any back who is kicking — that is, using 'the box', the small chip, or the grubber. The longer kicks are the problem of the backs and not the loose forwards.

The dummy halfback — The commonest dummy strategy is for the No. 8 to break off to create an extra man as halfback, or to drive forward to create secondary phase by letting in the loose forwards. These attacks can only be mounted if there is a stable scrum. The No. 8 cannot detach himself to pick up the ball (if he is the first man to pick it up, and generally he will be) unless the scrum is stable and moving forwards. If the scrum is going backwards and that move is called, the No. 8 must pick it up and take his chances — there is no point in passing.

Let us assume that the No. 8 is going to pick up the ball and pass it to the halfback. The No. 8 pushes first, and when the ball has come back to him he takes out one opposition player and passes to the halfback. Whichever way the play goes, the open-side flanker or the blind-side flanker becomes the immediate supporting loose forward, and the other loose forward comes around the back of the scrum to support that move. If it is the No. 8 who is to receive the ball from the halfback, it is a more difficult exercise and one that I do not think should be used as much as the traditional one where he takes the ball himself. One reason against it is that he cannot push as well. The No. 8 has to move out to play dummy or to play first five-eighth (which is in fact what he is doing); he is off the scrum too soon, and the effectiveness of a very strong No. 8 is lost. If you intend to use the No. 8 as a battering ram at first five-eighth, you must assume you will lose scrummaging power.

The No. 8 can push, pick up the ball and pass, or he can push, pick up the ball and run. Those tasks are easier to perform than asking him to be the first five-eighth with the halfback passing to him.

Defence against the Wyllie-type move — Correctly executed, the Canterbury/Alex Wyllie move is almost infallible — though it has been less effective in recent years. I think Canterbury over-use it and are therefore predictable in certain areas of the field. In defence you should certainly coach your loose forwards to combat it; you should tell both your flankers that a 'Wyllie' could run either side. Wyllie's great value, before we devised ways of stopping him, was that he could run either way, that he stood square behind the scrum, and therefore had both options open to him. Both flankers need to be on the alert to tackle a 'Wyllie' as soon as he moves; the interceptor has to be the flanker, no one else is capable.

Whichever way he runs, the flanker becomes the critical defensive forward initially, with quick and very immediate support from the No. 8. It must be a holding tackle for the ball near the line. If you can hold him and the ball, you have performed well. Hold him with the ball and push him back, then you've performed exceptionally.

If you are a good attacker, you take a flanker out of play by forcing him to tackle, and then spin and put the ball on to your own flanker, who is coming up in support, meanwhile aiming to create a gap between your opponents' halfback and first five. The great value of that move is that at least you create a strong, attacking maul and you have not lost the ball.

If you have got the ball in your scrum and your opponents are pushing you backwards, you need to clear the ball quickly. You must coach your side — particularly if you know they are not competent enough to hold a strong scrummaging side — that the ball has to be put in as soon as you make contact with the opponents. Put in the ball and let it travel straight through your scrum. Do not fumble around with the ball in your scrums; do not give the opposition a chance to become settled. It is the speed of your formation, and the accuracy and speed with which you can attack the opposition and move the ball in and out, that are the most effective ways of opposing a very competent scrum. Certainly it is not the three-man scrum — a waste of time and an admission of failure and incompetence.

If you can win a push-over try, it is one of the finest achievements because another forward pack has been eliminated. The best players to do it are the loose-head flanker — because the ball should be somewhere in front of his eyes — the No. 8, or the halfback, who is probably the most effective because he can see it and he is not pushing. Once you go for a push-over the whole eight need to push very hard, and thus the halfback becomes the player best able to score.

The loose forwards' role — Any specialisation in the loose forward positions — for example, blind-side/open-side flankers — should be opposed. I believe

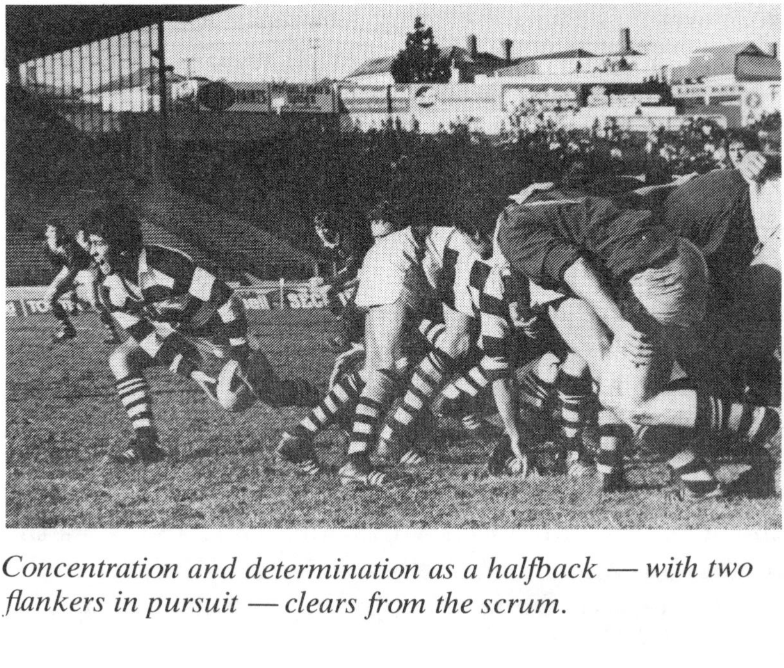

Concentration and determination as a halfback — with two flankers in pursuit — clears from the scrum.

it is far more important to talk about loose-head and tight-head flankers if specialisation is necessary. The loose-head flanker pushes differently from the tight-head flanker; he sees more of the ball on his side's put-in and much less of it on the opposition side's put-in. He needs to concentrate on watching the ball go through the opposition's scrum, as it is difficult for him to see it. The loose-head flanker will also find that the opposition halfback runs his side most often — it is the natural side for him to run.

I feel that ball-handling skills are becoming more important for loose forwards. This is partly because the maul is increasing in importance, but it is also because new rules have created a situation where there is more flow and the forwards frequently get into the backline. This means that loose forwards more often have the chance to run on to the ball when it is carried by backs.

Loose forwards are ineffectual unless the tight forwards are functioning properly. There is no way that the flankers can leave the scrum if they are going backwards. If you are struggling all the time to hold the opposition in set play, particularly in long, hard scrummaging, you certainly won't be an effective loose forward.

There is a maximum time for pushing in the scrums. Loose forwards must be sensitive to this — they must learn when to stop pushing and start concentrating on defending and attacking.

Wheeling the scrum — I think you need a well-formed scrum to start talking about wheeling the scrum. When we win the ball, I believe we want to win it going forward and going straight forward; and the less wheeling motion the better, unless it is a planned move from the scrum.

There is definitely a place for wheeling the scrum on the opposition's put-in, effectively stopping forward movement. This tactic also brings your halfback and flanker around onto the opposition scrum-half. Wheeling the scrum can also be an attacking move, especially close to the opposition line when it pushes the opposing halfback and flanker away from the ball.

A dive-pass to avoid the opposition halfback.

The Powerhouse Scrummaging Machine

While the conventional scrum machine is an excellent idea in theory, in practice it has a number of limitations, and a new machine, recently introduced to the New Zealand market to overcome these drawbacks, is sure to be successful.

A conventional machine allows only a horizontal pushing action with no provision for vertical movement — a most important factor in set scrummaging, one which is a potential cause of back injury and therefore requires specific coaching to eliminate.

Furthermore, the conventional machine does not simulate the movements of an opposing scrum and therefore does not teach many of the crucial scrummaging techniques. It also requires considerable ballast, whether by an opposing pack, backs, or a wall, post or tree. The resulting damage to grounds has become the bane of many a groundsman.

The Powerhouse Scrummaging Machine is actually a four-in-one unit offering coaching facilities for set scrummaging, rucking and mauling, as well as weight training.

The scrummaging section consists of two pads connected to a leverage and pushing collar system, allowing simulation of the pushing points of a real scrum. It allows props to move up and down independently as their position in the scrum requires, while the hooker adopts a realistic position between them. Padding is designed to be comfortable, allowing players to raise their heads and so encourage correct back posture.

The leverage system works against a quickly adjustable resistance, and the props raise and lower themselves against a measurable force. This means it can be used for specific neck and back strengthening exercises. As well, the height and width of the pushing collars can be adjusted to develop more scrum thrust

and to suit players of *all* grades. The hooker has ample space in which to operate, without injury and a clear view either side.

The Powerhouse moves on rollers that will not damage the ground, and can be ballasted with sand or water, thus eliminating the necessity for an opposing pack. Brakes can be applied to the rollers for greater resistance. The front roller is pivoted for development of wheeling techniques.

At the front end of the machine is a rucking and mauling pad, so all important coaching factors can easily and effectively be covered in any training session.

Lineouts

A lincout is the means of re-starting play when the ball has been put into touch. The fundamental skills of the lineout — throwing, jumping, catching, supporting, and feeding the ball — can be practised both as individual or unit skills. Eight forwards and a halfback co-operate to make the lineout an effective means of gaining possession. Each player in this group has a specific task and must be committed to carrying out this task.

If props are to be selected for their scrummaging strength in addition to their all-round mobility, then locks and at least one loose forward will have to be selected for their jumping ability.

The hooker, flanker or wing three-quarter may be the best lineout forward in the team. He must be able to throw the ball accurately for each lineout jumper in the team. How he throws the ball will depend on the position and style of the jumper.

The halfback co-ordinates all moves between the backs and the forwards. In the lineout he must think about the type of ball the backs require, the strengths and weaknesses of both his own and the opposition lineout, and the team's tactical approach to lineout play.

The jumping forwards in the lineout are numbers 2, 3, 5, and 7. When not jumping to catch, they should adopt a supporting role. The player jumping to take the ball should always aim for a two-handed catch, which will give maximum control.

The law relating to the lineout should be studied because it has a bearing on the positioning and repositioning of players.

Lineout signals are the responsibility of the halfback and can be verbal or non-verbal. Whatever system is devised, the signals should be simple and easily understood by the players.

The team's intentions in a lineout should be kept from the opposition, even though some changes in body position are necessary depending on where the ball is to be thrown.

The aim of every lineout, whether a 'feeding' or a 'driving' lineout, should be to go forward. A forward gain of one metre is often sufficient to allow your backs to operate efficiently.

The basic features of a lineout can be practised by using five players.

The Feed

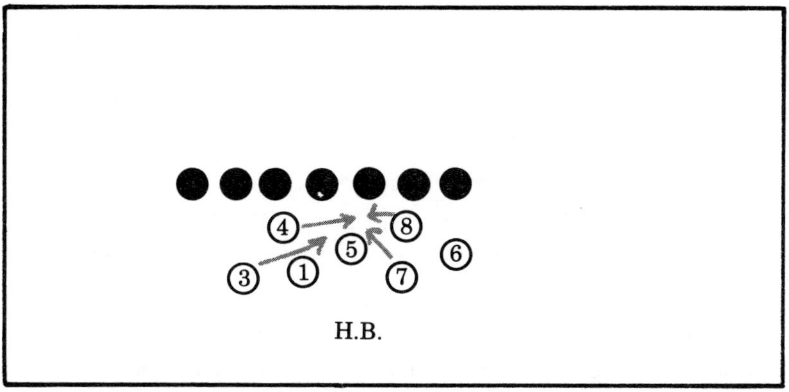

- No. 5 has taken the ball.
- Both players on either side have taken up a supporting role.
- All players form a wall to prevent the opposition interfering with the ball.
- All players have moved forward pushing the opponents backward.
- No. 5 has feet apart with knees bent and ball held clear.

The Drive

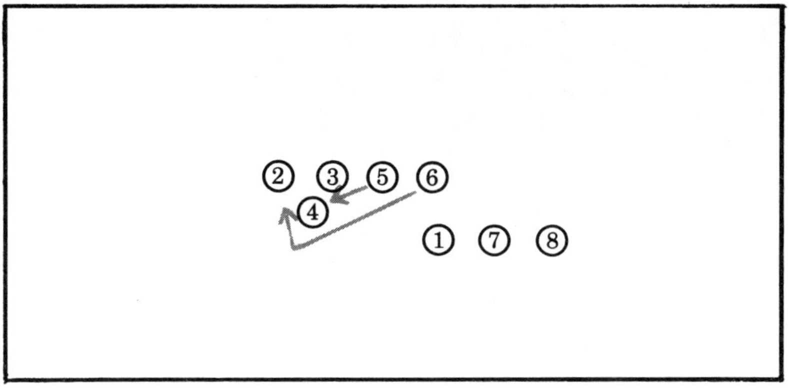

- No. 3 has taken the ball.
- No. 2 and 4 are supporting No. 3.
- No. 5 is moving into the gap between No. 3 and 4.
- No. 6 is moving into the gap between No. 2 and 3.
- The whole formation has moved forward.

Whether feeding or driving, the ball can be thrown to 2, 3, 5 or 7. All players except the jumper will be required to apply their weight and drive to the lineout in the correct manner.

Each player has a job to do, but this varies according to where the ball is being thrown. Ensure that the supporting forwards know their precise role when driving.

1. *Catching* — Mid-air catch and throw. The catcher stands with one foot a little in front of the other (the

A good two-handed catch.

front foot is the foot nearest the centre of the lineout, that is, the line of touch), knees slightly bent, hands by the sides, eyes on the ball. The jump is timed so that the ball is taken with outstretched arms at the top of the leap. Hands should be about 30 cm in front of the face so that the ball can be seen at all times. The palms of the hands face the ball, fingers are spread, thumbs almost touching. Immediately the ball is caught, the trunk is twisted to face the halfback. At the same time the arms swing down to deliver the ball with a strong wrist action to the waiting halfback.

It is important that:

- The hooker's throw really stretches the jumper.
- The jumper times his leap correctly.
- The hooker holds the ball high so that the jumper can see the ball.
- The jumper twists early enough so that he may better deliver the ball to the halfback.

2. *Land and pass* — The leap, catch and twist are as in (1). As soon as possible the ball is pulled into the stomach. The landing is made with feet astride, knees bent, and rounded back towards opponents. From this position a quick pass can be made to the halfback. Check that the jumper achieves a stable balanced position on landing so that he cannot be turned or upset by the opposition.

3. *Hold and drive* — With this method powerful support is required from the rest of the pack. The jump and the catch are as described in (2), but the catcher lands so that he may drive his shoulder into his opponents. The ball is snapped down onto the hip, while supporting team-mates bind into a maul. Encour-

age the jumper to drive hard with his shoulder for the nearest gap in front.

4. *Guide back — Two-handed guide:* At the height of the spring the tips of the spread fingers of both hands guide the ball towards the waiting halfback.

One-handed guide: Although a jumper can reach much higher with one hand, this method tends to lose control. The jumper should use the outside hand because the opponents find it far more difficult to obstruct. The outside hand reaches up to the ball with the elbow slightly bent and the palm of the hand facing the halfback. The ball is trapped by the hand and guided down to the halfback.

As a variation the jumper can guide the ball to another forward in the lineout who is able to take it and give a two-handed 'feed' to the halfback. Make sure the ball is trapped and guided, not slapped when the one-handed guide is being used. When guiding to another forward, make sure that the other forward has not prematurely buried his head in a supporting role.

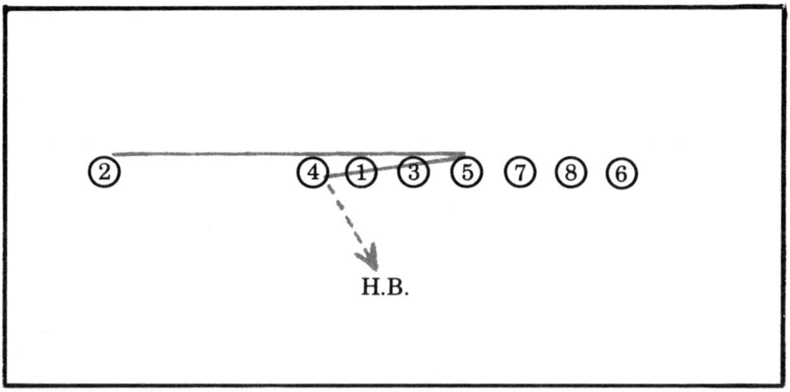

Variation on the one-handed guide.

Throwing

The quality of the lineout play is often determined by the throw from the hooker. Hookers or wingers must know the type of throw that suits each jumper and practise to perfect that throw.

The position of the jumper in the lineout has a bearing on the type of throw used. The throw to a No. 7 jumper needs to be a high lob in order to clear intervening forwards, but the throw to a No. 2 jumper might be low, flat and hard.

There are two throws used: the over-arm and the spiral. When using these throws, the hooker holds the ball high so that it is visible to all forwards in the lineout.

The over-arm throw — Feet are astride and at right angles to the sideline and outside it. The ball is held high above the head with the fingers of the throwing hand curled round the end, the forefinger making contact in the depression where the seams meet. The fingers of the supporting hand rest gently around the forward point of the ball. The weight is on the front foot and the eyes are on the point of aim.

The body weight rocks onto the back foot. At the same time the throwing arm swings back with the forearm assisting in the support of the ball. The arm swings down to about a metre away from the thigh. The free arm is extended forward and upward as a guide.

The throwing arm now swings up and over to deliver the ball at full stretch. The free arm swings down and back the whole action being like a cricket bowl. The trajectory can be changed by altering the point of delivery; the earlier the thrower releases the ball, the higher the trajectory.

The spiral throw — The left foot is right up to the sideline in advance of the right; the thrower is front on to the lineout; the ball is held about 60 cm in front of the head with the arms slightly bent. The fingers of the right hand are curled round the right-hand side of the ball close to its near end, and the left hand supports the left-hand side near the far end. Body weight is slightly forward and eyes are on the point of aim.

As the ball is carried back above the head, the body weight is transferred onto the back foot. As the throw is made, the left hand acts as a support and the right hand follows through to the point of aim, spinning the ball to the right. This spiral spin on the ball helps it retain its line in flight. The trajectory of the ball can be varied by changing the angle and point of release.

All moves from the lineout depend on the quality of the throw, and practice, understanding and concentration are necessary.

Allow the thrower and the jumper to discuss the type of throw to be used. With an average of 50 lineouts in a game, winning a lineout from your own throw should be regarded as just as important as winning a scrum.

Establish how far the thrower can throw with accuracy. Younger players may have to limit their attempts to 2, 3 and 5 in the lineout.

Practices

Throwing — Each thrower should practise throwing for accuracy.

- The player walks along the sidelines of the field, throwing the ball so it lands on the sidelines.
- The player stands on the goal-line and aims to hit the nearest upright of the goalpost with his throw.
- The player aims his throws at marked targets on a wall to achieve a fast, flat throw or a lob.

Work in pairs, one as a marker, the other a thrower. The marker starts at a No. 2 position and then moves to No. 3, 5 and 7 positions. He stands on the centre line of the linout, i.e., directly in front of the thrower. When the marker stands at the No. 2 position the thrower attempts to make this throw pass about 30 cm above his head and between his extended arms. When the marker stands at positions 3, 5 and 7, the thrower attempts to lob the ball directly to or just behind him. Change places.

Leaping for height — Player stands and leaps to slap as high as possible on a marked grid. This exercise is designed to strengthen thighs and ankles and gradually increase height.

As the lineout forward is not expected to make a vertical jump, he should practise jumping in from about 30 cm away from the wall, touching the wall with the back of hands, and landing with back to the wall. Foam-rubber sheets or some form of padding against the wall will help take the impact.

It is difficult for a forward to jump in a lineout when there are other players in close proximity, particularly when some are bent on obstruction rather than clean possession. Most good lineout jumpers have had supporting forwards who have made it possible for them to carry out their skills unimpeded. Some lineout

jumpers tend to move forward into the ball on the catch, and others move back. At this point jumpers should practise with support forwards as much as possible.

Turning the catcher — Forwards can work in two groups of four. Jumpers 2 and 3 should oppose each other in one group and jumpers 5 and 7 in the other. Spare forward to throw the ball. The hooker throws for No. 3 jumper to take the ball. No 2 and his supports make no attempt to jump for the ball. As No. 3 lands with the ball No. 2 spins him around, and his supports tear the ball away from him.

Attack from lineouts

Attacking from lineouts is most important, as this is the only time that the opposition's backs have to be 10 metres behind the advantage line.

The outside backs should generally be the key players in any attacking moves from a lineout. The first five-eighth is likely to be confronted by the opposition's No. 8, and I would often use the fullback as extra man. I do not think the blind-side winger is used enough from lineouts, and when he does come in, it is too close; I prefer to see him coming at least outside the second five-eighth, if possible outside the centre. On gaining the ball from the opposition's throw-in, the halfback or first five-eighth kicks the ball into the 'box' for the blind-side winger to chase. Other methods are centre doubling outside winger, or fullback coming outside winger.

Driving around the end of the lineout from a 'tap down' ('Willie away') is a good attacking move. The No. 7 should be used unless the No. 8 is tall. If you have no tall players at the tail of the lineout, you can throw the ball right over the back so that the last lineout player can move back to catch it. A variation of this move is to have a drive straight on No. 7, who has caught the ball and brought it down.

The front of the lineout is also a good place to attack from. Using a short throw to No. 2 and the drive on No. 2 by the other forwards. Also try a quick throw to No. 2 and then a 'tap' back to the thrower.

Any moves from lineouts by the backs should

generally be made by outside backs, and there are many variations that can be worked out for the forwards. The key to the success of these moves is an accurate throw to the lineout jumper. One variation of the quick throw-in is seen where player 13 has picked the ball up from in-touch and, before the opposition arrives, has thrown the ball in to a team-mate.

Lineout attack from the quick throw-in.

Defence from lineouts

In defence from lineouts everybody should know where they are going and whom they are marking. The front of the lineout is covered by the thrower who should try to catch the opposing halfback so he cannot break down the blind side. The No. 8 should try to catch and disrupt any opposition backline movement towards their first five-eighth by keeping on the inside and forcing him out. Those forwards not involved in jumping for the ball should try to get through the lineout to put pressure on the opposition's halfback. No. 7 in the lineout must make sure that the halfback does not run before heading off among opposition backs.

All backs should come up to mark their opponents, keeping slightly on the inside of them. If they bring an extra man into the back line, each player in the lineout moves in one, so that the overlap is on the outside, and the opposition's extra man is covered by your fullback (your blind-side winger covering their fullback). The halfback does the job a No. 8 would do from a scrum — that is, covering behind the backs.

Conclusion

- Because lineouts take place along the touchlines, the team gaining possession has the whole width of the ground in which to operate.
- By spinning the ball quickly along the backline to the winger or extra man in the line, the attacking team attempts to penetrate where the opposition's defence is thinnest.
- As a general rule, from the quick feed from the lineout

the thrust comes from wide out.

- The second five-eighth or centre must straighten before passing the ball on.
- At lineout practices the open-side wing three-quarters should receive the ball when in line with the goalpost. Naturally, in the game the backs will be forced across.
- Encourage the second five-eighth to stand slightly wider and run square.

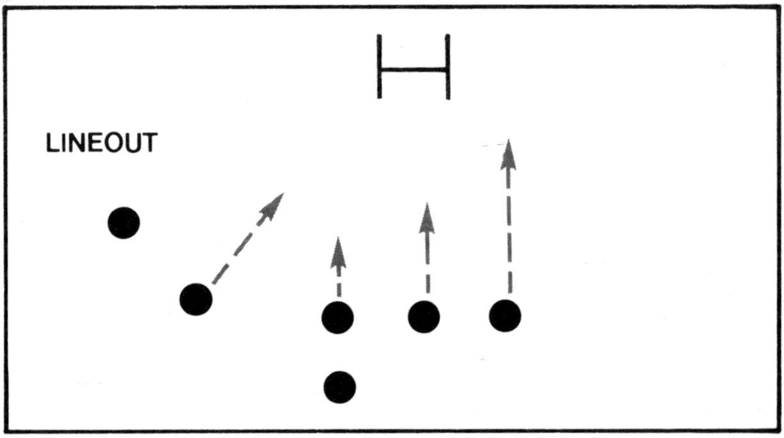

Second five-eighth to stand slightly wider and run square.

The Maul

Two important principles of play are support and continuity. The maul and the ruck are both strategies that enable the ball carrier to maintain possession for his side and thus open a number of attacking options.

The first decision the ball carrier has to make is whether he should engage in contact or distribute the ball. Players must be encouraged to develop running and passing skills that may make contact in a particular situation unnecessary. Sometimes mauls are deliberately set up, but usually they develop as a result of physical contact with an opponent, particularly in a tackle. In modern play, apart from lineout mauls, backs are usually involved in the formation of the maul platform. They must therefore understand the basic techniques and must be confident about contact in the maul structure.

Forming the maul platform — It is at this point that the great debate develops. Remember that it is vital to secure possession of the ball. The attacking options will depend very much on the initial platform that is formed and the binding method used by the support players.

The appropriate technique in formation depends on the number of players immediately available to support the ball carrier, who on impact turns to his support.

The first and second players to arrive in support of the ball carrier should go to alternate sides and bind on to and over his back. They form a protective wedge on each side and can drive into the opponent. By binding, they help keep the ball carrier on his feet and maintain their own stability. They form a broad and strong base on which to build a maul.

Other support players bind on so that there are two or three men on each side of the ball carrier in an arrowhead formation. The ball is usually released back through the clear channel to the halfback and there is a straight feedback from a wide frontal platform. This type of platform is sometimes developed from lineout play, but it tends to be rather static, with no driving forces coming in behind the ball carrier and the first

Support players form a secure platform from which the ball can be safely channelled back out to the halfback.

Forming the maul platform: Ball carrier turns to face his support.

First two players bind in on alternate sides against ball carrier, onto and over his back.

two support players.

In order to establish a strong driving force, the third and fourth support players wedge themselves between the ball carrier and the first and second support players as if they were locked in a scrum. The ball can either be fed to the 'locks' or put on the ground. If the ball is handled by the locks, they can smuggle it back to another support player on the side of the maul or at the back of the maul.

It is crucial to develop the forward drive so the maul is dynamic and not static.

Principles of the maul are:

- Secure possession.
- Remain on feet, wide stance, lower hips.
- Drive the maul forward.
- Bind.
- Keep low body position.
- Keep eyes open.
- Control the ball back.
- Secure the flanks of the maul.
- Communicate.

Variations

Many coaches advocate that the second player, that is, the first support player to reach the ball carrier, drives on to the chest of the ball carrier, pushing him on and at the same time ripping the ball from him. The next two support players then wedge or bind on to the first support player. The maul is built with the locks coming in on each side of the first two support players.

In this strategy the ball carrier turns his back on the opponent, and the first support player takes the ball and backs into the original ball carrier. This has the advantage of moving the ball away from the opposition, but it also has the disadvantage of limiting the ability to drive forward.

Some teams prefer to have the ball carrier assume a half-turn (45 degrees), with the first support player going in on the other side at a similar angle. The two shoulders lock in to each other, that is, left shoulder to left shoulder, or right shoulder to right shoulder. Other support players tend to build the platform on the sides of the first two players. So long as the transfer has not been made to the first support player, the second and third support players can bind or wedge on to the original ball carrier. The advantage of this technique is that a wide frontal arrowhead is formed. It also allows a clear channel back to the halfback.

The rolling maul — The rolling maul is a recent development that provides another attacking option. The ball carrier drives into the opposition and sets up the ball by backing into the opponent. The first two support players bind over the ball carrier, creating a protective wedge on each side. A wide frontal platform is usually developed.

A support player takes the ball from the original ball carrier, but instead of feeding it back to the halfback, he rolls off the maul and, supported by another player, drives forward at the opposition. This explains the technique in its simplest form. Careful practice can develop a more effective concept.

Assume that the ball carrier No. 1 makes contact with an opponent and turns and reverses into him. The first two support players, Nos. 2 and 3, go to alternative sides and bind on to and over the back of the ball carrier. They face the opposition and bind on to their respective opponents with their outside arms. Support players Nos. 4 and 5 come in between players 1 and 2, and 1 and 3 respectively, as if locks in a scrum. As player No. 6 approaches the maul platform, he determines the side on which to develop. If he wishes to develop the roll to the left side, he binds on the left-side lock with his left arm (the outside arm on the body of the left lock). He can then take the ball from ball carrier No. 1 with his right arm (the inside arm), while applying force against the opposition.

When the opposition has the ball — It is essential that an opposition ball carrier be tackled and turned bodily in the tackle, so that the ball will lie within your part of the maul as it is formed. The next player to arrive will assist with the turning of the ball carrier and will form the driving platform or wedge on the side opposite to the initial tackler. As the rest of the forwards arrive they will supply the drive through the normal maul platform formation.

A well-secured maul platform is difficult to counter, and it is usually impossible to get at the ball itself. However, you can ignore the ball and keep the opposition's ball carrier and support players on their feet, endeavouring to drive their maul platform backwards. If all your players are bound together and committed to the drive, then it is sometimes possible to gain the advantage of momentum over the team with possession while its players are concentrating on the transfer of the ball.

If the opposition ball carrier cannot be turned to expose the ball, it may be possible to drive his feet from

Support players shield the ball carrier from opposition players in a ruck following a successful lineout take.

under him. This requires a low driving impact on his legs at or below the back of the knees. As the ball carrier falls to the ground into the opponents' side of the maul, defenders can isolate his support by driving in and over the ball-carrier, thus developing a ruck situation.

There are not many mauls that require more than five or six players. Hence your team, as the defending team, may benefit from having the last one or two players position themselves on either side of the maul, ready to latch on to any opposition players who peel or break away. Players on the defending side who are stationed at the back of the maul should be encouraged to unbind and 'roll' to the direction of any wheel or peel, thus achieving the same result as a defensive player who positions himself for a tackle without ever joining the maul.

Drive forward — All players should attempt to move the ruck forward for the following reasons:

- If your side drives over the ball and frees it, the halfback has a stationary ball to pick up, rather than one that moves erratically from a misdirected heel.
- If the ball is won by the opposition, they receive it in the worst possible way, i.e., going backwards.
- When you win the ball from a ruck going forwards the opposition backs are usually going back and moving in close, which allows your backs to operate more freely.
- If the ball fails to come free from the ruck, you stand an excellent chance of gaining the put-in from the ensuing scrum.

Remain on feet — All players must remain on their feet in a ruck. Any player who collapses on to the ground obstructs the course of the ball or upsets the purpose of his team mates.

Control the ball back through the ruck — This is best done by going past the ball, driving over it, and moving the whole ruck forward, leaving the ball a still target for the halfback. If the feet have to be used, a gentle controlled movement with the ball of the foot, not the heel, is best. Players must understand the halfback's need for a controlled ball.

A forward who uses one foot to rake a ball has reduced his pushing power by at least 50 per cent.

Secure the flanks of the ruck — The last two forwards to the ruck form up on its sides so that if the opposition wins the ball, these forwards are in a position to harrass the opposition's backs.

Comparing the ruck with the maul — Coaches debate at length the relative merits of ruck and maul. The team of today must be adept in both. It is poor coaching to suggest that the team will only ruck or will only maul; there will be ample opportunity for both during every game.

Teams may well have a preference and endeavour to create ruck situations rather than mauls. The physique and technique of the players and the position of play in relation to the gain line will usually dictate the method to be used. Genuine rugby is applying the correct technique at the correct time, and this is particularly important in the ruck and the maul.

As a general rule, if the attack is developed quickly into the opposition territory and ahead of the attackers' gain line, quick possession is desirable. In a ruck the ball is left on the ground or is propelled back along the ground while the players in the ruck structure move forward, over and ahead of the ball. Generally, this gives the advantage of quicker possession of the ball for the backs.

The ruck allows a more powerful drive forward, thus committing more of the opponents' forward pack and causing the defensive backline to realign more hurriedly. Hence, some coaches advocate a ruck when play is going forward and quick ball is needed.

Conversely, if defenders have to track back to stop a driving attack behind their own gain line, they need time to regroup and their backs need time to form a new defence line. In such circumstances there are advantages in slowing down the momentum and feed by creating and developing a maul.

By varying the pattern of the maul structure, the speed with which the ball can be delivered from a maul can also be varied. If a maul forms across the gain line, the ball can be ripped or transferred quickly from the original ball-carrier and passed through a clear channel to the halfback. On the other hand, if players have to track back to a maul behind the gain line, it is more effective to wedge and drive, thus slowing down the delivery of the ball.

The maul has some advantages over the ruck. The ball can be screened from the opposition and it will usually be difficult for the opponents to see it. It offers safer possession with better control by hand and foot. The attacking options are greater. The ball can be worked back to the last man, who can peel away like the No. 8. It can be worked to the sides for a breakaway attack on the flank. The maul can be screwed like a scrum and the ball rolled away with players turning inside-out, binding in twos for maximum protection and drive. Finally, it can be easily converted into a ruck.

Because they can achieve better control, many teams set out to maul their own ball. If the opposition has the ball, there is advantage in concentrating on the tackle and the ruck to rob the opposition or to deny it controlled ball.

The maul and the ruck must be used to exploit possession, position and pressure, going forward to score tries. They are not ends in themselves, but are to be developed for their attacking potential. Once the attacking advantage has been obtained, the ball should then be presented to the team's backs to exploit that advantage.

Rucking

A ruck is a loose scrummage and is distinct from a maul because the ball is on the ground. Forwards may be in any position in a ruck. It is quite usual, because they are first to the breakdown, for the loose forwards to be at the centre of the ruck, with the hooker in a flanker's position.

Rucks can take place in any position on the field, and it must be remembered that the forwards will have to go back to rucks as well as forward. In practice, forwards should learn that it is vital to move to defensive rucks. In an attacking ruck the opposition's defence tends to be disorganised, and in a defensive ruck your own defence may be in disarray and vulnerable to the opposition's attack should they secure possession.

A maul may be turned into a ruck by putting the ball carrier on the ground.

The key to good rucking is for forwards to position themselves quickly and approach the ruck from behind.

Secure possession — This may be achieved by dropping on the ball, by tackling and robbing the ball carrier, by carrying the ball into the ruck situation, etc. Any forward setting up a ruck must be aware that possession is crucial; the ball must be isolated from the opposition as quickly as possible.

Maintain low body position — The incoming player should assume a low position at least two metres from the ruck, aiming at knee level. This will bring his shoulders level with the bottom of the shorts of other members of the ruck.

Ruck parallel to the touchline — Any forward momentum should be directed towards the opposition's goal-line. A forward who enters the ruck from the side not only negates forward drive but also destroys his own team's control of the ball.

Ensure that players come into the ruck in depth and are not assisting the opposition by driving in to the side of the ruck.

Bind — All players must bind in a ruck. The shoulders act as the battering ram, the arms pull inwards, and the drive and thrust come from the legs. Players use shoulders and arms to bind and drive.

Keep eyes open — Eyes must be open and players fully aware of the ball's position in the ruck.

Practices

Building up the pack — Pair A runs and rucks into pair B. On 'break', pairs A and B move in and ruck against

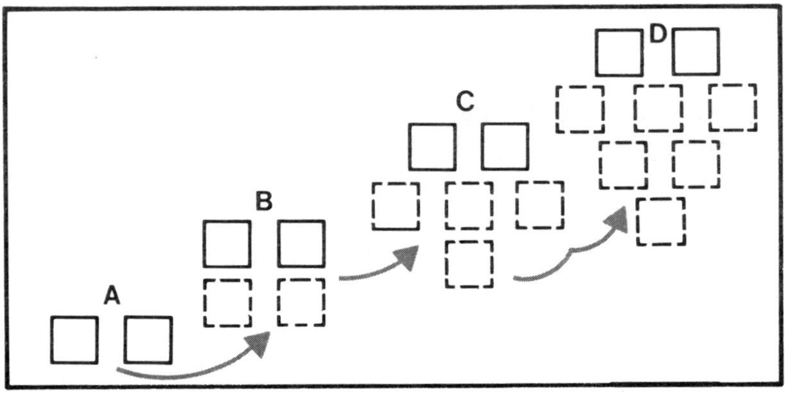

pair C. On 'go', pairs A, B and C ruck into pair D. Rotate groups so that each pair starts from A's position.

Driving practice (groups of five) — The middle player assumes a low body position and drives into the two players he is facing, then turns and drives into the two players behind. Emphasise hitting low with shoulders and binding with arms.

Attacking rucks — Place rugby balls diagonally up the length of the field. The eight forwards start in the corner of the field and run towards the first ball. The first man to the ball picks it up and turns, while the rest of the pack drive into him. He drops the ball back on the ground and they ruck. On 'break', the pack breaks and moves to the next ball.

Defensive rucks — Place rugby balls in position. Forwards practise as outlined, except that on 'break' they now move back to the next ruck. Insist that the first forward snaps up the ball and moves shoulderfirst into the opposition. Defensive rucks must be driven hard towards the oncoming opposition.

Supporting the ball carrier (groups of three)— Players jog down the ground. On 'ruck', the ball carrier turns, and the two following players drive in on each side to support. The ball carrier rolls the ball back along the ground and one of the supports turns, picks it up, and becomes the new ball carrier. Repeat. Encourage the ball carrier to hold the ball low so that supports assume low driving body positions.

Ensure that:

- Players understand the need to get the ball two

players away from the opposition.
- Supporting players keep the channel to the halfback open.
- Only two forwards actually handle the ball.

Spin the ball-carrier (groups of four) — A holds the ball. B moves in quickly on A, grasps him round the upper part of the body and spins him round. C and D quickly move in to take the ball away from A. Repeat, changing roles.

The Backline Unit

In many ways the backline is the most undercoached unit of the team. Many coaches spend time with the forwards, but tell the backs to work out their moves and practise a bit of passing. In some situations the backline can easily play to a pattern; in other areas of broken play it requires a high degree of instinctive reaction, awareness and spontaneity. In these departments especially, backline coaching becomes a real challenge. Now let us examine some of the fundamentals of this important unit.

The ultimate aim is, of course, to score tries, but the immediate aim should be to cross the gain line. If you can do that, you are getting closer to the scoring position and making it easier for the forwards to contribute to the continuity of the attack.

There are three elements involved in carrying the ball past a certain point: the distance to be covered, the time available, and the pressure put upon you by the opposition. For a backline these factors are governed by the four P's:

- Possession.
- Position.
- Penetration.
- Pace.

Possession

The aim of the game is to score tries and to do this it is necessary to have the ball. The set scrum, lineout and kick-offs give us an advantage to win the ball, so from set play on our ball these skills need to be practised again and again.

Having won the wall, the backs must have the skills to out-manoeuvre their opposition and at the same time retain possession. Backs, then, aim to pass and back up; to kick and regain possession; to maintain continuity of forward movement; to use individual elusive skills and to out-think the opposition with the hard-earned ball they get from the forward unit.

Possession from opposition ball from their set plays is through constant pressure upon the opposition by screwing the scrum; the eight-man shove; harrassing the halfback; contesting the throw-in at lineouts, and tackling opposing backs before they can reach the gain line. These tactics can earn us second phase possession which is excellent ball if we are positioned correctly to take full advantage of it.

Position

The back division must understand collectively their positioning for both attack and defence.

On attack — One of the most effective formations is the 'banana' positioning where the players are standing five metres apart in staircase formation such that each one is able to see the jersey number of the player inside. The backline is fairly flat with the banana shape resulting from a slightly deeper first

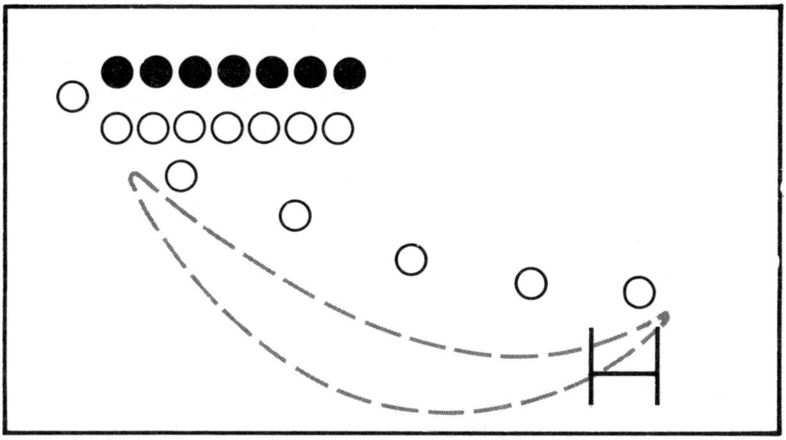

five-eighth and a slightly shallower open-wing position. This positioning makes it easier to get close to the gain line before encountering the defenders.

The first five-eighth should not begin to run until the ball is in the halfback's hands. The other backs in turn will accelerate onto the ball, while running along a straight line in a strict one-versus-one situation.

All backs must keep their eyes on the halfback, as he is a key man in all phases of play. Do not move until the player inside you moves. Do not 'creep', keep your depth.

Another common set-up is a very deep formation where the principal aim is to give real space to the outside backs, the fullback and the supporting blind-side wing. This still requires very quick hands and confidence in the penetrating ability of the players out wide. These players will receive the ball well behind the gain line, but should have some 10 to 15 metres in which to outmanoeuvre their opponents.

In a variation of this the five-eighths and centre stand much closer together than the normal passing distance of five metres. This allows them to have the same advantages of acceleration and space without starting off so far behind the gain line. In this case the centres can accelerate by fanning away in an arc as the ball approaches. They must then step in and straighten before they pass.

With these conventional alignments the backs need to be conscious of the difference between their starting positions and their receiving positions. It is pointless to assume chosen positions if all the players move into a totally different line before the passing really starts. The key man to retain available space for the line is the first five-eighth, and he should not set off at least until the pass from the halfback is on its way, and often not before it is in his hands. It follows that the rest of the backs should take their starting cue from the first five-eighth.

The standard positioning that has been described can be modified to allow extra attacking options. As an example, the inside centre can be given a lot more thrust if he is dropped behind the line to form the apex of a triangle with the first five-eighth and outside centre. This thrust would be ideal for linking up with a halfback who has run around the five-eighth. Even in defence, this positioning tends to encourage an outside break from the opposition five-eighth, thereby creating a breakdown close to your own pack.

Three-tiered attack — This can be used where groupings of first and second five-eighth, blind-side wing and centre, fullback and open-side wing allow the majority of the backs to really burst onto the ball from all angles — important in wrong-footing the defence.

Coaches should be encouraged to try innovative and radical forms of alignment. Not all are original, but they have seldom been tried at a sufficiently high level of rugby to make them generally acceptable.

Three-tiered attack.

Box formation — The traditional position of a backline almost demands that the ball be thrown across the field. This is fine if it produces space to penetrate or extra support for an overlap, but it is usually difficult for a backline to create space out wide from a scrum.

The Australian-style box formation has proved effective for this. It gets its name from the positioning of the first and second five-eighths, and the centre and open-side wing. Because of their flatness, the first and second five-eighths must stand still and pass quickly to give the deeper support time to run onto the ball before the tackle line is reached.

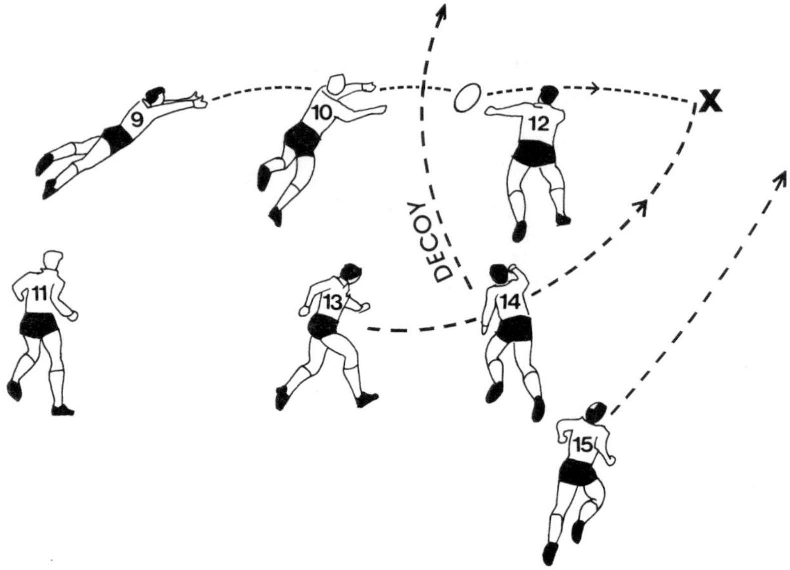

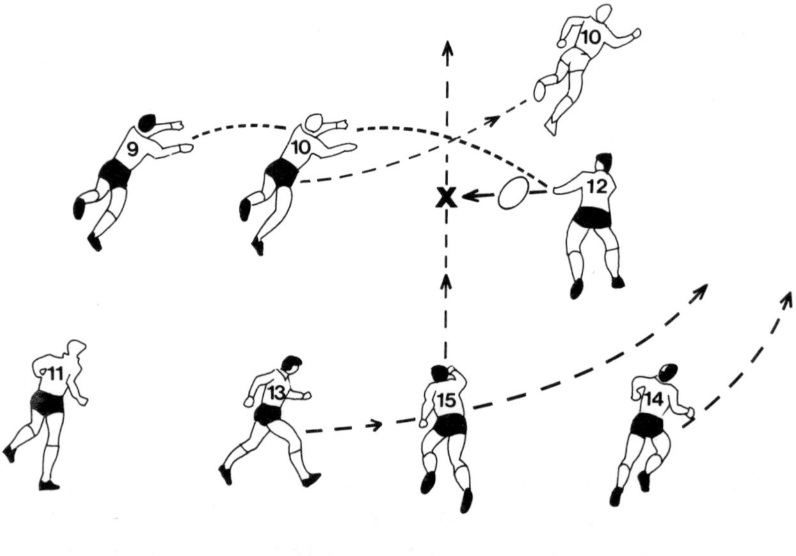

Variations of play from Australian-style box formation.

Other variations in positioning for backline movements from set play:

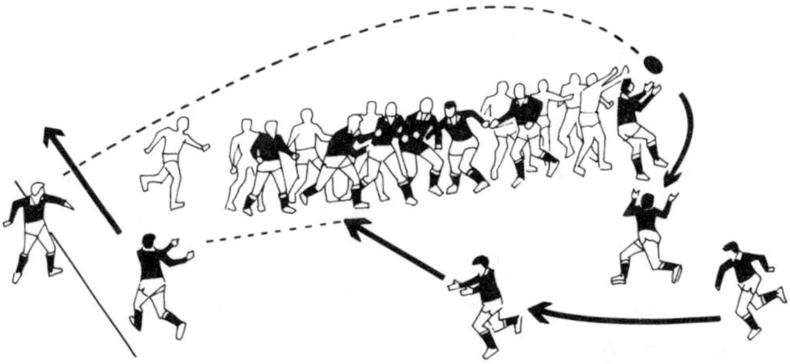

From a long throw the ball is reversed to the first five-eighth running blind, who passes to the wing or links up with the forwards.

The No. 5 taps to a No. 7 running the blind, who sets up a maul or drive, or passes to the halfback or wing.

From a short lineout the flanker (or halfback) gets the ball running wide and then passes to the wing on the blind side.

Penetration

Because defenders come up on the inside shoulder, and because backs tend to run on an angle across the field before receiving the ball, there is a tendency for backlines to take a long route to the gain line. This is pointless because it not only contravenes the principle of going forward, but it also reduces the space and the time necessary for penetration by the ball-carrier and all those outside him. The straight approach angle has the advantage of committing the defender to one man, thus destroying his thrust onto the outside ball carriers. The benefits of good angles are demonstrated in the following diagrams.

Straight approach gives ball carrier the option of an inside or outside break and commits tackler to one man.

Across-field angle by ball carrier allows defender to partly cover two men.

The opportunity to straighten is much greater in midfield, especially at the position of inside centre or second five-eighth. Normally the halfback does not run at all, so the angle starts from the first five-eighth position.

As an alternative the first five-eighth can anchor himself and catch and pass without moving, but unless he stands deep, he is an easy target. However, this method does have the effect of committing the inside defence away from the three-quarters and is particularly appropriate for some of the unorthodox alignments previously mentioned.

Another option is for the first five to move across-field on the run, into the direction of the pass, to give him and his immediate supports momentum for the outside break or half-break. This allows the halfback to throw a longer and more lobbed pass and gives the backs a good line for the jink inside. The longer pass enables a speedy backline to clear the ball away from the pressure of the opposition backrow, but has the disadvantage of making it difficult to straighten further out. Even if a break is made while running across field, this angle is not really effective because it gives the cover-defence too good a target for a break.

Keeping the problems of the five-eighth in mind, we can now see that the responsibility for straightening often comes from the inside centre. He can achieve this by positioning himself behind the projected receiving point and running straight onto the ball, or he can approach that point obliquely and step inside onto a straight line as he takes the ball. This is best done by swinging his body slightly away from the direction of the pass. It is wise to use both methods for variation. Once the inside centre has established the correct path forward, the outside backs can easily angle themselves onto him and use the space he has created.

Apart from making it easier to beat opponents on the inside and outside, straight running also helps the ball carrier to break through tackles. It provides for a greater range of vision and makes it a lot easier to link with the forwards. When second-line players are introduced into the attack as extra men, the position changes somewhat, because a change of angle is often necessary in this situation to break the defence.

The only way to reach the target of the gain line is to penetrate the defence. This can be done by:

- Creating overlaps.
- Creating gaps.

• Individual elusiveness.

Overlaps are usually created by support, and gaps are usually the result of deception and individual skill. The introduction of an extra man, with attention to the insides straightening before they pass, is a basic move to create an overlap.

Players will never become effective at beating a man in a game unless they are given opponents to beat at practice, and all coaches should remember this point.

The individual skills of players will no doubt help a backline to penetrate the opposition. These should be taught and encouraged. Some evasive skills are physical and may be used effectively by the more robust players, but others demand agility, that is, sharp, rapid changes in direction and pace. A combination of skills may be used to beat an opponent; a strong fend combined with a swerve can often effectively place the attacker out of reach of the tackler.

Penetration skills

The sidestep — For a sidestep to the left:

• The right foot takes a shorter stride, and a thrust to the left is made off its inner border. The right foot hits alongside or just in front of the left.

• The body weight is thrown to the left as the left foot swings sideways.

• The player picks up speed again quickly.

• At the moment of execution the ball may be transferred to the left arm, leaving the right hand free to fend, or the ball may be carried in both hands to aid the deception, e.g., to allow for a dummy pass.

Sidestep about to be executed by an expert. Note the good support he has in case of trouble.

A shortened stride creates better balance for the player, thus allowing him to change direction quickly. It is often necessary to slow the pace before a sidestep can be executed effectively.

The player should be aware of the danger of a number of consecutive sidesteps which bring him closer to the converging cover-defence. Any movement that causes a cut-back against the run of play should be followed by a swing out to enable the attacker to link up with outside supports.

The prop — For a prop to the left:

- Going to the left the player pushes off the right foot.
- Steps are regular in length.
- The change of direction is not as abrupt as that developed by a sidestep.
- The body weight is thrown to the left as the left foot swings sideways.

This evasive method is often used by a slow-moving or stationary attacking player against a quick-moving defender.

The swerve — A means of avoiding an opponent that involves a change of direction and variation in pace. It requires good rhythm and balance, and an ability to change pace. A swerve is used to beat a player on the outside.

Using an outside swerve to beat an opponent.

- Players are moving at an angle to one another.
- The attacking player moves in towards his opponent in order to straighten his line of run.
- He then swerves away sharply to the outside.
- At this point the attacker accelerates.
- At the last moment the attacking player may place the ball under his outside arm in order to fend.

The fend — This involves physical contact, but can be used effectively by small as well as big players. The fend may be used by the attacker, either to push the defender away or to push himself away from the defender. The latter is generally used by smaller players. It is very difficult to fend a player who is approaching head on. The fend can be employed to best advantage when the defender is moving in obliquely or at right angles to the attacker.

The most effective fend is usually combined with a swerve, a sidestep or a change of pace:

- The attacker approaches the would-be tackler with fending arm bent (ball is carried under the arm furthest from the tackler).
- Timing is the essence of a good fend. At the critical moment the arm is straightened quickly.
- If the tackle is low, the point of contact may be the head or shoulder of the tackler; if it is high, the contact point is more likely to be the chin, face or chest.
- As the heel of the hand makes contact the arm is straightened.
- As contact is made the attacking player swerves away from the would-be tackler.

Make sure the fending player has his arm bent before the moment of impact.

The ball is carried in the outside arm as the attacker prepares to fend off a would-be tackler.

Ball carrier straightens arms at moment of contact with attacking player.

The bump — This is a tactic that uses physical contact to beat an opponent. Because the attacker is usually slowed down in the process, it should not be attempted unless absolutely essential.

The bump may be used against an opponent approaching from directly in front, obliquely, or from the side. It is probably easier to bump an opponent who is using a low tackle than one who is tackling high:

- As the attacker approaches the tackler he crouches.
- On impact the attacker hits the would-be tackler with his hip and runs on, usually at a much reduced speed.

Ball carrier crouches in preparation for evasive 'bump' — getting ready to hit with the hip.

Breaking a tackle — Many attacking players submit to tackles far too easily. They have the initiative because they are carrying the ball, and the defender is often badly balanced and apprehensive about his ability to halt the oncoming attacker. The attacker must strive to break clear of the tackle by driving with his legs until he hits the ground and is finally held. Many half-hearted tackles can be broken if the attacking player has developed the ability to spin in tackles. He should spin towards the weakest point of the tackle — where the tackler's hands meet. Impress on the attacking player that his forward momentum is not finished until he has been grounded. All players should know that using the space behind them can be the most effective means of avoiding a tackle.

Practices

(1) *Four teams* — Players, each carrying a ball, move off four at a time. They run at half pace over the first 10 metres, sprint over the next 10 metres, and return to half pace over the last 10 metres. Return by reversing the process.

(2) The group jogs down field. On 'patter' players run on the spot. On 'right' or 'left' players sprint in that direction. On 'jog' players straighten up again.

(3) Practise sidestep at slow walking pace, slow running pace and fastest possible pace.

(4) *One against one* (use a grid) — A and B run towards each other. A carries the ball and sidesteps B, either to the right or left, before B can touch him.

(5) Using half the 22-metre area. Have three players as defenders and the rest as ball carriers. Each ball-carrier in turn attempts to touch down over the goal-line. He uses all evasive methods to beat the defenders, who attempt to touch him on or below the shorts as he progresses towards the goal-line. The ball carrier with the least number of touches is the winner.

(6) *Fending* — In pairs. A and B move down the field side by side, B carrying the ball. On 'tackle', A turns to tackle B, who fends and moves on. Progress from walking to jogging to running at half pace.

(7) *Bumping* — In pairs of comparable size. B carries the ball and stands close to A, who assumes a position as if to tackle low (head behind B's hip and arms spread). B lowers his body and bumps, and A tries to force him back. This is a difficult skill because of the solid physical contact necessary.

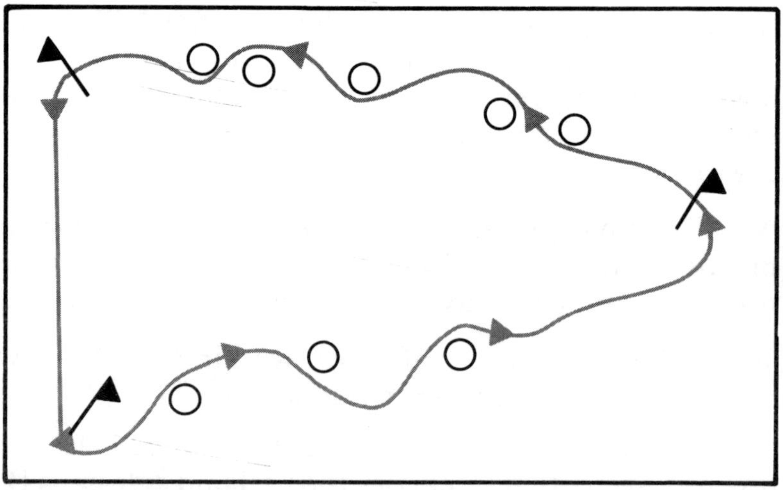

An elusiveness course.

Set up a regular course to practise elusiveness — Three posts 25-30 metres apart to form a triangle. Position more markers along one side for sidestepping, swerving and propping, and along the other side for sprinting and dummy scissors. Leave one side free for sprinting and other practices. Have three players at start positions, each with a ball in hand. Hold the ball in two hands and change from one to the other for the various activities. Have small groups of players at each point for a relay.

Pace

Running speed is only one aspect of backline pace. The simplest way to beat the opposition to the gain line is by sheer speed. If you see you are not going to make it in a straight line, you must quickly move the ball onto another path where you have a better chance. Other aspects of backline pace are passing speed and thinking speed.

Running speed — It is necessary for backs to do a lot of sprint training to acquire genuine running speed. The five-eighth is in a difficult position because he is under pressure, so he needs the licence to be able to steady himself while receiving. He must show real speed off the mark because the effectiveness of his few steps before passing depends on acceleration. The three-quarters must then burst onto the ball with some acceleration while the ball is in the air. If each player does this, he will be moving at sufficient speed to take advantage of a gap should it present itself. Normally he will pass the ball as soon as he receives it, but if he

Running with the ball in two hands enables the carrier to easily re-distribute the ball if tackled.

decides to make the big thrust forward and reach the gain line himself, he does not necessarily have to maintain full speed for that run.

Passing speed — The standard for passing speed is to be able to pass the ball in one or two paces. A ball that is being carried both on the run and through the air must outspeed a running defender. Any form of attack is based on the transfer of the ball from a point of untenable pressure to an area of vulnerable defence, and the speed of transfer depends largely on passing, which must be secure and quick. The quickness comes when backs, in particular, begin to feel the ball as an extension of their arms. This can only develop from continually having the ball at their fingertips during practice, and being exposed to situations where they must unload it quickly, no matter which foot they happen to be on when they receive the ball. The hands must go out to meet the ball, and the pass has to be thrown in front of the receiver.

Thinking speed — The back usually has a choice of passing, running or kicking, and his decision must be made quickly to avoid losing space for productive running. It is just as important to be able to count four of your men against three of theirs as it is to be able to run fast or pass quickly. However, unless it is a classic two-versus-one situation where a man has to be drawn, the decision should never be 'run to the man and then pass'; it should be 'pass and support' or 'run and try to beat the opponent'. Good decision-making will only come from experience gained by practising with some form of opposition.

Function of the backline unit — The halfback and first five-eighth shape the pattern of play. The scrum-half is a key man at the lineout and must decide whether the won ball should be fed back or driven. He must also liaise with the forwards, informing them in which direction he and his fellow backs are going to move from the set scrum. In the main, play tends to pivot round the halfback and first five-eighth. Thus it is important that these players work together as often as possible so that a close understanding of one another's play begins to develop.

In all moves where a player has been missed out, he should back up to take another pass and maintain continuity.

Main aims

- Make room on the outside of the backs by moving the ball quickly. Quick feed from lineouts — look for the penetration on the outside because it is much easier.
- Use the short side or blind side from scrums, but take the ball flat.

• Create an overlap by using an extra player — fullback, blind-side wing, No. 8 or a player doubling.

The dive in the corner completes successful backline movement.

Rugby Skills — Individual and Group Practice

Tackling

Tackling requires determination, courage, confidence, timing and balance.

There are essentially three types of tackle: side-on, frontal and rear. On the field of play these are usually executed as: side-on (low), frontal (low), frontal (high), frontal (smother), rear (low) and rear (smother).

A wise coach sets aside time at training sessions to develop the players' skills in the art of tackling and being tackled. The results will show in fewer injuries and fewer points for the opposition.

When a tackle is properly executed both tackler and ball carrier can absorb the physical demands and pressures without injury and can even enjoy the experience. Tackling is a skill that is available to each and every player — more so than other eye-catching skills — and provides an excellent medium for all players to make a positive contribution to the team effort. Properly executed, the tackle is a joy to behold. Ill-conceived efforts such as head-high tackles, foot trips, stiff-arm tackles, scragging, and even ankle taps, bring discredit to the skill itself, as well as to the player, team, coach and the game.

Players should think of tackling not only as a defensive skill but as a means of attack. The tackler who puts one of the opposition down behind the majority of his own team-mates sets up an ideal counter-attack situation. All players should be aware of this and strive to make their tackles behind the advantage line. The further the opposition is allowed to move over the advantage line, the more the tackle becomes defensive.

Although the low tackle is to be highly commended, there are other methods that will sometimes achieve a more satisfactory result. The low tackle close to your own line could result in the opposition scoring. Whatever method is used, the defender's main aim should be to halt the opposition's attack by stopping the man with the ball, and to prevent him getting a pass away.

Practices should be carefully supervised to ensure that there are no injuries. Grade the practices for tacklers and teach static positions before moving into more dynamic, forceful movements. Coaches should also emphasise ways in which the tackled player can make the ball freely available for his own players.

Not exactly copybook, but it works!

Practices

There are varying opinions on the value of practising tackles when the players are moving at pace and with power. Coaches usually find it difficult to motivate team-mates into tackling one another at practice sessions, but there will certainly be some sessions during the season when it may be warranted and will be worthwhile.

Tackling can be practised and improved by a combination of two methods:

• Players actually tackle each other, but they are kneeling, and either static or moving only slowly. This allows greater understanding of the actual techniques.

- Players work out hard on tackling bags or rubber tubes. This allows development of power, pace and confidence.

Kneeling tackles — In pairs, both players (ball carrier and tackler) kneel, ball carrier holding a ball. Tackler is at right angles to ball carrier's line of movement. Tackler now falls gently into the side-on tackle. Repeat a few times, then reverse roles. Then reverse again and again to give both players the opportunity to tackle with the other shoulder. As knowledge and awareness of the mechanics is gained, more drive can be generated by the tackling player.

The next stage is to have the ball carrier moving — both players are still on their knees. This makes the tackle more realistic. Repeat the changes in roles and shoulders. From the kneeling position players can advance to a walking pace and then a jogging pace.

Tackling bags — Tackling bags and the rubber inner tubes of tractor tyres are valuable training aids, which allow players to generate power, pace and confidence once the mechanics of the tackle have been clearly understood. Individual players can practise alone with the tackling bags.

To encourage the players to use speed, effort, knowledge and fitness in a high-pressure situation, games can be devised for the training session. Here is a tackling-bag relay:

Two teams line up. Ten metres in front of each team is a tackling bag held up by a player. Ten metres farther in front is a football, or marker (again, one for each team). The player at the head of each team's line sprints forward, tackles the bag (at this, the bag-holder returns to become last in the team's line), sprints on to the football (or marker), rounds it, and runs back to pick up the tackling bag. Then the second tackler can move off, tackle the bag, up and around the football, and back to the bag.

Using rubber tubes — The rubber inner tubes of tractor tyres offer an interesting and valuable variation. When they are bowled they are very similar to the movements of a ball carrier and can be tackled from the front, from the side and from the rear. A blob of white paint on the side of the tyre can provide a focus so that players can time their side-on tackles accurately. Work in pairs for all types of tackles. Make sure the tyre valves are safely covered.

Four players (A, B, C and D), each with a rubber tube, stand at the corners of a large square. A fifth player (E) is within the square. The object of this exercise is to see how many tackles player E can make in, say, 20 seconds. Player A bowls a tube to player E, who tackles it. B's tube is bowled and tackled, then C's tube, then D's tube. A, B, C and D sprint to retrieve their tubes after each tackling and return to their positions ready to bowl again, and so on until the 20 seconds has elapsed. A and E swap places and it is A's turn to tackle the tubes.

The side-on tackle

The tackler's role:

- Do approach the ball carrier at an angle to keep your opponent running one way.

- Do use your right shoulder if approaching from the left and vice versa.
- Do make the tackle as and where you want it.
- Do aim to strike the middle of your opponent's thigh (midway between waist and knees); with your head to the side behind.
- Do not watch the ball carrier's hands or body movements; watch his legs and feet.

Side-on tackle: Head of tackler should be behind ball carrier's legs.

The ball carrier's role:

- Do carry the ball away from an intending tackler.
- Do lean your body into the tackler — sometimes swing your hip or buttock into the tackling shoulder.
- Do consider the use of a fend, swerve or sidestep to avoid the tackler.
- Do relax your body as you fall if the tackle is successful.
- Do try to turn and present the ball (either on ground or on your body) to team-mates.
- Do use your free arm to help break the fall (if possible).
- Do not keep the ball in the stomach area as you fall.
- Do not forget to release the ball immediately it touches the ground.
- Do not forget that you must be up and on both feet to play the ball.

The frontal low tackle

The tackler's role:

- Do place your head to one side, adopt a crouched position, head well forward, legs well bent, and back rounded. Eyes open all the time.
- Do encourage a moving opponent to run into your shoulder.
- Do try to get your knees and head on the same side of the ball carrier.
- Do try to wrap the ball carrier's knees tightly with your arms and allow the ball carrier's momentum to carry both bodies back and down.
- Do retain a rounded back and perform backward roll (which can prevent the back of your head from hitting the ground with any great force).

The ball carrier's role:

- Do try to drive in with your hip or lowered shoulder, with the ball held away from the tackler.
- Do ensure that your body twists and that the ball is presented to your team-mates.
- Do drive your legs with power to break the tackler's arm-clasp.

The frontal high tackle

The tackler's role:

- Do try to make the tackle high, endeavouring to lock the ball carrier's arms firmly against his body with the ball well locked between.
- Do hold on tightly with a strong grip.
- Do cushion your fall by spinning or turning the ball carrier, who will then take the impact on the ground.

The ball carrier's role:

- Do drive with power through the tackle.
- Do use a low shoulder to effect penetration, with a possible lift at the time of impact.
- Do twist and present the ball to team-mates.

The frontal smother tackle

The tackler's role:

A frontal smother tackle is required in open-field play, when endeavouring to ensure that the ball is not passed on in a two-to-one situation.

- Do make the tackle at the precise moment the ball carrier receives the ball.
- Do aim to lock the ball carrier's arms firmly against

his body with the ball well lodged in between.

- Do hold on strongly until help arrives, endeavouring to twist or turn the ball carrier towards your team-mates or, if power allows, drive the ball carrier into ground.

The ball carrier's role:

- Do endeavour to restrict the tackler's efforts to engulf the ball and your body in the tackle.
- Do try to keep the ball away from your abdominal area.

The rear smother tackle

The tackler's role:

The rear smother tackle is for occasions when the ball carrier has deliberately turned his back to the tackler to conceal the intended delivery path of a pass.

- Do strive to drive your chest onto the back (high) of the ball carrier with your arms around him, locking the ball and the body of the ball carrier together.
- Do slide your arms down to the ball area to restrict any pass.
- Do — if the occasion allows — drive your tackle 'through' the ball carrier, endeavouring to put him to ground with you finishing on top.

The ball carrier's role:

- Do try to get the ball down as low as possible and away from tackler's hands so that you can distribute it to your team-mates.
- Do try to stay on your feet and so present the ball to team-mates.

The rear low tackle

The tackler's role:

When the ball carrier is running hard for the goal-line and only a low tackle from behind will halt his progress, a rear low tackle is required.

- Do calculate the correct time to dive onto the ball carrier's legs.
- Do aim to make contact with the ball carrier's buttocks with your shoulder.
- Do use your left shoulder after a left-foot take-off, and your right shoulder after a right-foot take-off. Plan to tackle with your favourite shoulder.
- Do tuck your head to one side to ensure it makes no contact with the ball carrier's boots.
- Do wrap both arms around the ball carrier's thighs and slide down his legs.

The ball carrier's role:

- Do keep your thighs moving and the drive going full-tilt to break the tackle.
- Do use your free hand to break your fall.
- Do maintain possession of the ball where you want it for support.
- Do twist as you fall.

Using a rear low tackle to stop spirited progress to the goal-line.

Handling

One of the most important skills of the game is ball handling: picking up, carrying, passing and catching, and diving on the ball. Picking up a ball requires that the player has a low body position, relaxed hands and balance, and, above all, that he watches the ball carefully. Carrying the ball correctly makes more options available to the player. Passing should be rhythmic, controlled and well directed to allow the receiver to run onto the ball. While running to catch the ball, the receiver's hands should be still.

In all aspects of ball handling, balance and body position are vital. Use the flight of the ball to determine the position of your body. The ball carrier should pass the ball so that the receiver can catch it with as little effort as possible. To do this both players should be properly positioned.

Encourage players to carry the ball in two hands so that it is able to be passed either way.

Picking up

In the first stages of learning rugby it is difficult for a small boy to pick up the ball smoothly and correctly and run with it successfully. The teacher should emphasise that the ball is carried in the hands; the habit of tucking the ball under the arm should not be encouraged at this stage because it impedes passing.

The way a player picks up a ball will depend largely on what he intends to do with it. He may wish to pass laterally, run forward, or set up play for a closely following team member.

Stationary ball — To pass left he positions his right foot close to the ball, places his right hand behind the ball, completes the pick-up with his left hand, and steps towards the receiver with his left foot.

To run forward he places his right foot close to the ball, scoops with his right hand while the left completes the pick-up, and moves forwards.

When setting up play for a closely following teammate, he moves to the opposition's side of the ball to guard against a knock-on. He spreads his feet to give maximum stability and takes the ball up in two hands.

Ball rolling towards player — The action is similar to above if ball is moving slowly. The stride should be shortened, the approach slowed down, and the body placed behind the ball with the knees well bent. The back of the hand should be near or on the ground so the ball can be scooped up into both hands.

If setting up for team-mate following closely, the player should check momentum of the ball with hands, pivot body, placing back to opposition, and pick up in two hands.

Ball rolling away from player — Approach from the side, with the body well over the ball. If passing laterally, reach in front of ball to check its forward momentum, then position feet as for the stationary ball. If running forward, use a technique similar to that outlined for stationary ball. If setting up play, reach in front to check the ball's forward momentum, pivot body, placing back to the opposition, and pass or hand directly to a following team member.

- Insist that eyes are on the ball at all times, no matter where the opposition players are.
- Encourage a low body position, with hands as close to the ground as possible.
- The ball should be brought back towards the body after the scoop to avoid the possibility of a knock-on.
- A slower pick-up is far more useful than a very fast attempt, which often results in a knock-on.
- Unless this skill is mastered, poor handling will be the cause of many stoppages of play.
- There are times when the foot should be used rather than a pick-up attempted, e.g., near the goal-line with no opposition close at hand.

Practices

Relay — A sprints, picks up the ball, crosses the 10 m line, turns and sprints back, places the ball in the centre and runs past B. B repeats.

Pick-up drill — Players, in file of four, jog the length of the field. A carries the ball. On 'down', he places the ball on the ground. B picks it up and jogs forward, while A moves to the end of the file. Have a gap of two metres between players.

Pick-up for lateral pass — In pairs, one ball between two: B places ball on the ground and moves sideways across field. A moves into the ball, picks up and passes to B. In this way they proceed across the field. Return, with A placing and B picking up and passing.

Pick-up and feed (stationary ball) — Jog the length of the field. A places ball. B picks up, pivots, and hands on to C. Repeat with C placing and D picking up and handing on to A, who has returned to the end of the line.

Carrying

When the ball is carried correctly the attacking player has all options open, he can pass, kick or dummy easily, use the ball to confuse the opposition by letting it sway with the natural rhythm of his stride, or shift the ball from arm to arm to fend.

The ball is held in the hands, away from the body with the arms flexed at the elbow. Thumbs run parallel to the top seam, fingers are loosely spread and mainly in the bottom quarters of the ball. The point of the ball away from the carrier is directed upwards at an angle of approximately 45 degrees.

While the player is running, the ball swings naturally from side to side with the movement of the body.

Held in this position, the ball may be easily passed to right or left, lifted over a tackle, or its movement used to confuse an opponent. It may be tucked beneath either the right or left arm so that the ball carrier can fend. An attacker who has the defence coming at him from the left tucks the ball under the right arm and vice versa.

Both forwards and backs should carry correctly the ball at all times. The backs, particularly wing three-quarters, should tuck the ball under the correct arm when trying to beat an opponent. A relaxed carry will allow the ball to swing with the stride of the ball carrier, and players should be able to sprint at full speed without feeling the need to tuck the ball under an arm. Practise changing the ball quickly from the basic carrying to the tucked position.

Practices

Each player has a ball. Players jog from goal-line to 22 m mark, place the ball on the ground and jog on. On 'turn', players turn and sprint to pick up and carry the ball correctly back to the goal-line.

Relay — A sprints 20 metres to pick up the ball and carry it correctly back to B. B sprints to 20 m mark to place ball and return. Continue in this way.

Each player jogs with a ball. On 'right', the group sprints to the right; on 'jog' group straightens to jog down the field; on 'left' group sprints to the left. The ball must be carried in front, even when sprinting at maximum effort.

Relay — A sprints first 10 metres carrying ball correctly, tucks ball under right arm for second 10 metres, carries ball in front for third 10 metres, tucks the ball under the left arm for the fourth 10 metres and sprints all the way back, carrying the ball in front.

Touch-down — Requires one rugby ball, one hoop and two numbered teams, each behind a line four to five metres apart: The ball is passed along one of the teams, and on 'go', the player who then has the ball tries to run around his own team and ground the ball in the hoop before being tagged by his opposite number.

- The opposite number must run the same path as the player with the ball.
- A team scores one point for each successful touch-down.
- If the opposite number tags a runner, his team has the ball to restart the game.

Passing

Quick and accurate passing depends on the passer receiving the ball correctly, the position of his feet, his balance and rhythm, and the position of the player about to receive the ball.

It is necessary for rugby players to be able to give and take a variety of passes. For some players in the team one particular type of pass may be more common. For example, the halfback is expected to make a pass longer and quicker than any other player on the field, whereas the centre may need to develop a balloon pass in order to clear opposition players and allow his wings to run clear. A player receiving a pass must be moving in to the side and slightly behind the passer so that he can move up to take the pass correctly. This enables the passer to place the ball in front of the receiver so that it can be taken easily without interrupting his rhythm of his movement, and full use is made of his peripheral vision.

When the receiver is moving in line with the passer the ball is usually delivered onto his hip, a situation that causes the whole rhythm of the backline to be broken. A receiver running flat looks directly at the passer and thereby limits his field of vision. If the passer is taken out by a tackle, the flat receiver is past him before he can stop, and he is therefore out of play and unable to give the required support.

Encourage the receiver to run onto the ball and to reach towards the passer, and ensure that the passer delivers the ball in front of the receiver.

The ball is blocked by the hand furthest away from the passer, thus 'snatching' at the ball is impossible. The receiver must watch the ball right into his hands, which 'give' with the ball in front of the body.

Swing pass — Swing the ball smoothly across the body, turning the head, shoulders and hips to face the next receiver. Deliver the ball off the palms of the hands, using the fingers to give the final direction and height to the pass. To ensure that the whole attack has been straightened, the passer should, at the moment of delivery, swing in slightly towards his opposite number.

Passing to the right, the player delivers the ball with

his weight on the left foot and vice versa. When receiving a pass from the right, reach towards the passer, block the ball with the left hand, and complete the take with the right.

Ensure that the passer turns his head and shoulders when delivering the ball, and follows through with his arms and does not 'fling' the ball.

Under pressure, the ball carrier gets the ball away, his head, shoulders and hips turned in the direction of the pass.

Spiral pass — Most halfbacks use this technique because it gives added length and speed to the pass. All players should develop the spiral pass because, with today's emphasis on counterattack, long, quick passes are often needed to clear converging defence.

This pass is usually delivered from a static position. If the pass is being delivered to the left, then the right hand becomes dominant, with the left hand acting as a guide. The right hand spins the ball with the fingers imparting the final flick. The ball travels end-on, spinning in flight.

The halfback's pass — When passing from the ground the pick-up is made close to the foot furthest from the receiver. The foot nearer the receiver steps out in the direction of the pass, ready to receive the transferred weight. Arms and trunk swing the ball out in one sweeping movement. The dominant hand and fingers impart the spin.

A long, low-flying pass is aimed in front of the receiver's waist. Before the pick-up — so that he can make full use of his peripheral vision — the halfback should position himself so he is facing the opposition's second five-eighth. This enables him to direct his pass at the correct angle for his first five-eighth. Encourage the halfback to position himself correctly while waiting for the ball.

The ball must be swept straight off the ground. Ensure that the correct foot is close to the ball on pick-up — the right foot if passing left, left foot if passing right — and make sure that the lead-out foot moves towards the receiver. Encourage a low body position throughout the pass, and insist that the passer use his fingers to impart the required amount of spin to the ball.

The pivot pass — The techniques of pick-up and delivery are exactly the same as for the halfback's normal pass.

Halfback ready to snap out the ball and set the backline moving.

The halfback positions himself with his back to the scrum, lineout, ruck or maul. This method often allows the halfback a measure of protection for the ball, because his body is between the opposition and the ball.

Many halfbacks prefer to use a pivot pass when passing to the right, because their right hand is much stronger than their left.

Dive pass — Both the normal pass and the pivot pass may be converted into a dive pass.

The pick-up of the ball is made when the player is sideways to the scrum, lineout or ruck. The feet will normally be fairly close together and the body weight well forward. The pass is made with one long scooping action. The front leg straightens forcefully, projecting the body into a dive. The fall is broken by the arms.

This is a good pass to use in wet weather or when the ball is being chased by close-following forwards.

Balloon pass — This pass is used by centres who have the opposition wing running between them and their own wing.

The technique is as outlined for the swing pass, but the passer leans back a little and retains the ball in his hands longer so that the trajectory of the pass is high enough to clear the intervening player.

The overhead pass — This pass is designed to clear opposing players who are obstructing the path of the normal swing pass.

The ball is lifted above the passer's head and pushed towards the receiver by the hand nearer him.

Dummy pass — The movement of passing the ball is executed, except that at the full extension of the arms the player holds on to the ball and draws it back again.

Reverse pass — This pass can confuse the defence because it changes the direction of the play. The passer twists around as the receiver approaches and gives a short pass when he crosses behind him. Alternatively, the passer swings his arms as if making a normal pass but holds on to the ball and transfers it with reversed hands as the receiver crosses behind him.

Long pass — A long, flat pass may be used, which gives more thrust to the ball, missing out a team member and putting another player into a position of advantage. This also allows less time for the defence to be effective.

Short pass — This pass is often used by forwards who wish to transfer the ball back to an oncoming team member.

The passer moves hard into the tackle and turns to pass the ball directly back. Equal emphasis is given to both hands when delivering the pass.

The supporting team member should be positioned in depth on the ball carrier so that he bursts onto the ball, giving thrust to the attack. A low, aggressive body position should be assumed by both the passer and the receiver.

Variation: The passer retains possession of the ball, and the receiver actually rips the ball away from his team-mate. The passer holds the ball at about hip level, and both players assume low, aggressive body positions.

Practices

Pressure practices:
One circle competing against another, all players facing outwards. The winner is the team that completes the circuit first, or the team that achieves the greater number of passes in a set time or without a drop.

Figure of eight — Two even teams spaced around circle so players are at least three metres apart: Each leader has a ball. On the signal the balls are passed around the circles. Last person in each circle passes it to leader of opposite circle. When a circle is without a ball, that team scores a point. Leaders then start again, this time with the opponents' ball.

Moving practices

In pairs — The passer is stationary. Partner walks (later jogs or runs full speed) and takes the pass. Proceed across field, paying attention to footwork.

In threes — Pass at full speed, paying attention to the receiver's position. In this practice the middle player must pass to both left and right. Change centre player so that all have a turn.

In fours — Pass at full speed. Place markers, and check that players veer in towards these as they deliver their passes.

Pressure practices

Relay of four — The first four players in each team set off down the grid, passing their ball. When they reach the other end they return, still passing. The next four then take over. The first team to finish wins.

Backing-up drill (in fours at the end of the grid) — No. 1 acts as halfback and gives a spiral pass from the ground. This sets the players away. No. 1 then runs across behind the other players as they move up the grid, in an attempt to touch the last receiver before he reaches the other end of the grid.

Rotate players so that they all have a chance to practise the pass and to back up.

Variation: No. 1 uses a variety of passes, e.g. pivot, halfback, spiral.

Three versus seven (two grids) — A has the ball and is supported by B and C. The attacking team can run with the ball but must pass after having been touched on the shorts three times by three separate defending players.

The defending players can move only back and across, always keeping behind the ball. Their function is to keep an 'in-depth' screen, covering the ball-carrier.

The attacking players continually 'back up' the ball-carrier trying to penetrate the screen.

This practice allows players to set up an attack during broken play when players from both sides are all over the field.

Four versus four (use a grid) — The side with the ball attempts to score a try by passing and backing up. An attacking player must pass when touched on or below the shorts. The attacking team loses possession if the ball is dropped, passed or knocked forward, or if players run out of the grid. Once an infringement occurs the ball is given to the other team, both teams return to their own end of the grid, and the game begins again. After a try has been scored the ball is always given to the other team.

Two versus two (short pass) — A carries the ball and moves down the grid. C tackles A, who passes back to B. B is tackled by D. B passes back to A, who scores at the end of the grid.

This practice may be extended over two grids with a greater number of tacklers and an equal number of passers.

Variation: The same practice may be used with the passer turning and presenting the ball (at about hip height) for the supporting player to rip out of his hands as he drives forward.

Corner ball (use a grid) — The attacking team tries to corner one of the opponents and tag him. The attacking team must not run with the ball. A player must retain the ball in his hand while making a tag. Any tagged player drops out. If attacking team drops the ball, a tagged player may return to the game. Defending players must not intercept the ball or run out of the grid. Each team has three minutes in which to make its tags. The number of tagged players outside the grid at the end of this period represents the score.

Deceptive practices (use a grid)

Three versus one — A carries ball. A, B and C proceed down the grid. D touches A, who has timed his pass to B. B passes on to C, who scores at the end of the grid.

Two versus two — A is the ball carrier. A and B proceed down the grid. C touches A, who has passed to B, and D touches B. Meanwhile A has doubled round B to take his pass and score at the end of the grid.

Missing the double — A carries the ball. A, B and C proceed down the grid. E touches A, whose pass has gone to B. A doubles round B. D touches B, F comes up to touch A, but B misses A and passes on to C, who runs free to score at the end of the grid.

Reverse pass — A carries the ball. A moves straight at C, committing him to the touch. B runs behind A, who passes to him. B scores at the end of the grid.

Variation: C now shadows B. A makes out to pass to B but retains the ball and runs on to score.

Catching

All players in the team are at times under pressure to catch a high dropping ball, a skill that requires concentration and ability, and also demands a fair measure of courage. This situation often occurs when the opposition is kicking off or when they are endeavouring to attack by means of the high 'up-and-under'. In both these cases the opposition is often bearing down rapidly on the catcher. The catcher should position himself so that the ball will land just in front of his chest, and should move to that position quickly so that he is still and well balanced to take the ball.

A stable stance is most important. The catcher has one foot forward and arms raised with palms up, forming a cradle with the chest. His eyes are fixed on the ball, and his upraised hands should be within his field of vision. As the ball enters the cradle, his knees and hands give, his hands clasp firmly over the ball, his elbows tuck into his trunk, his body curls forward over the ball from the hips, and the ball is hugged to the chest. Relaxation is critical.

Many players turn their bodies to the side as the ball is taken so that:

- The ball is kept away from charging opponents.
- The catcher can readily drop his shoulder into an oncoming tackler.
- The catcher is less vulnerable to a crash tackle.

- In the case of a misfield, a knock-on penalty can be avoided.
- The catcher is well placed to kick for the line.

Under intense pressure, a defender making a clean catch can gain relief for his team by claiming a 'mark'. To do this he must be standing still with both feet on the ground and must call 'mark'.

At times during a game it is essential for the catcher to leap off the ground to take a two-handed catch above the head. This often occurs at a kick-off, during lineouts, or when players from both sides are clustered beneath a high kick. The technique in this case is very similar to that used by a forward jumping in a lineout.

Ensure that the catcher anticipates where the ball will land and moves quickly to that spot so that he can assume a stable and balanced catching position. It is important that the arms are raised to co-ordinate hand, eye and ball movement and the knees are bent at the moment of catch for maximum relaxation. Make sure that the catcher positions himself side-on to protect himself from tacklers and check that he quickly transfers the ball to a carrying position so that he can run with it, pass or kick it.

Static practices

In pairs — The ball is thrown high for partner to catch (thrower uses one of the lineout throws), or the ball is kicked for partner to catch.

Time ball (use grid) — A, using a lineout throw, sends the ball to B. B catches and passes back to A. B bobs down. A then throws to C, who catches, passes back and bobs down. This practice is continued down the line. When E catches the ball he runs to A's position, while A goes to the front of the line.

Variations: Use as a pressure practice, or throw the ball over the crossbar of the goal post.

Moving practice (use a grid)

Relay catching — A throws the ball into the air in front of the line. B sprints forward to catch and then takes A's place, while A runs to the end of the line. The thrower must try to make the catcher sprint into the ball.

This may be used as a pressure practice with one team competing against another.

Kicking

Each player should be able to kick with either foot because at some time he will be faced with having to use his less dominant foot.

Kicking, if performed accurately, can be a most effective means of attack.

Because the modern rules of rugby do not always allow a defending player to kick the ball directly in to touch, such kicks must be made with much more precision and accuracy.

In a successful rugby team there should be specialist kickers: players to take penalty kicks to touch on either side of the field, place-kick specialists, and a player to handle the halfway kick-offs and 22-m line drop-outs. The players selected to carry out these kicks should practise them. The player who takes a 'mark' under pressure and must kick to clear should be well prepared.

The punt — The ball is held pointing in the direction of the kick, with the upper hand spread on the top side of the ball. The V made by the thumb and forefinger of the upper hand should cradle the end of the lace nearest the kicker. The lower hand steadies the ball by supporting in front and to the side of the upper hand. The player must keep his eyes on the ball until after the kick.

The non-kicking leg is forward, ready to take the body weight as the ball is kicked. The kicking leg is drawn back, and the ball is released by the lower hand. The upper hand guides the ball down as the kicking leg swings forward.

The instep (laces of the boot) connects with the curved surface of the ball just below its widest portion. Contact is made immediately after the knee straightens. On contact, the foot is well stretched (toes pointed).

The kicking foot follows through. Body weight is well forward, and the kicker lifts up onto the toes of standing foot.

Ensure that the kicker:

- Uses the correct grip.
- Guides the ball down onto the foot.
- Contacts the ball with the instep.
- Points the toes of the kicking foot.
- Has his head down and follows through correctly.

The short punt — This kick is used by an attacking player in order to pass an opponent without being tackled. The player must be able to recover possession before the opponent can turn round.

The short punt should be practised on the move, as it

is usually made on the run. The follow-through should be sufficient to carry the ball to the nearest open space, a short distance in front of the kicker. Ensure that the kicker does not kick too early.

Spiral punt — Because of its streamlined trajectory with this kick, the ball meets less air resistance than in the orthodox punt and is airborne much longer.

The spiral spin is imparted with a slicing action by rolling the foot across the ball. At this point the kicking leg will be straight and the toe pointed. It is important that the kicking foot is drawn slightly across as the foot makes contact.

The up-and-under — This high kick gives the attacking team time to reach the landing spot at the same time as the ball. It is like a normal punt, but the ball is directed high into the air because it is hit later with the kicking foot, which follows through to a much higher position. Aim for height and distance.

The grubber kick — Practise this kick in a stationary position as well as on the move. The kick is made along the ground and usually through a gap in a line of defenders.

The ball is held as for a punt and dropped end-on as for a drop-kick. The instep and shin hit the ball just before or as it hits the ground. The knee is well forward over the ball, and the action is a short one, almost a stab.

At the end of the kick the toes are still pointed down. The ball skims along the ground for a short distance. It is important that the knee is well past the ball at the moment of impact, and the kicker forces the ball into the ground.

Pivot kick — This kick is similar to the punt and is generally used in a defensive situation when a player (for example the halfback) has to kick for touch because he is crowded and facing in the wrong direction.

The ball is contacted higher than usual, which means that it is released well away from the body. To make sure that the ball is safe against charge-down or interception, the kick has a high trajectory and goes outside or over the shoulder. The follow-through should be high enough to place the ball out of reach of opponents.

Encourage the kicker to be in a position to protect the ball from oncoming opponents.

Drop-kick — Grip the ball as for the normal punt. The ball is dropped end-on and at a slight angle to the ground, a little in advance of the non-kicking foot. The instep of the kicking foot swings through to contact the ball as it bounces up.

The follow-through is directly after the ball, with body weight forward and head down.

Some players tend to approach the ball obliquely and make contact with a hooking action.

For a run-up take three running steps.

It is important that:

- The ball is dropped correctly.
- The kicker's eyes are on the ball and his body well over it.
- The kicker is well balanced to make the kick.

Place kicking — Two methods are used:

- Direct approach (a) ball placed upright, (b) ball lying down (torpedo kick).

• Oblique approach (round-the-corner kick). Ball placed upright on a mound.

Two types of hole are used.
• Round hole — for short kicks. The heel is driven into the ground and then screwed round.
• Banked hole — for the torpedo kick, which is for long distance. With back to the goal, the heel is hacked into the ground to make a U-shaped bank. The ball is placed into or above the hole at the required angle. For long kicks a flat position is usual.

Aim for the middle of the posts, even in a slight breeze. A good kick should tumble backwards and hold its line. It is the back spin that holds it on line.

Check that the kicker:
• Takes time to make a well-constructed mound for the kick.
• Walks back correctly.
• Realigns himself before he begins his run-up.
• Watches the position of his non-kicking foot.
• Does not aim too far away from the centre of the posts.

Direct approach — The player starts with feet together near the ball. He walks back and stands with feet together in ready position. The goal is sighted and any adjustment to the approach is made. His eyes are then fixed on the ball, concentrating on the spot where the toe will make contact. The kicker then rises on his toes and runs up in a straight line to the ball. The toe of the kicking foot connects with the lowest portion of the ball visible. The ankle is stiffened and the non-kicking foot is placed alongside the ball.

The follow-through must be straight. Use the arms to assist balance.

Oblique approach: His eye on the ball, and his leg starting to straighten for the impact.

Oblique approach — Place the ball upright as outlined earlier. When kicking from the left, aim the ball about one metre inside the right-hand post. Determine the flight path as shown. Walk back a suitable distance. Try to make the walk an extension of the flight path to the post, as illustrated.

Place the non-kicking foot beside and a few centimetres away from the ball. Hold head steady, eyes firmly on the ball, and strike the ball, toe down, through the midline of the ball. Power is achieved by an explosive straightening of the leg on impact, and there should be a full follow-through along the line of flight. Kick with the laces.

Practices

Punting:

Individual — Practise holding and lowering ball onto a foot. Punt the ball into the air so that it can be easily regained. Use both right and left feet.

In pairs (five metres apart) — Players punt to each other along a line for accuracy.

In pairs (10 metres apart) — A rolls to B, who moves in, picks up the rolling ball and punts it back to A. Repeat with B rolling the ball.

In pairs (five metres apart) — A punts to B. If B makes a clean catch, he steps back one pace. B then kicks back to A, who also steps back one pace on making a clean catch. If the ball is dropped by either player, he takes a step forward. The pair furthest from the start line are the winners.

First player in team A kicks to first player in team B and sprints to the end of team B. First player in team B kicks to the first player in team C and sprints to the end of team C. First player in team C then punts to second player in team A and sprints to the end of team A's line.

Kicking for accuracy — Each player has a ball except E, who is placed to recover kicks. Players in turn kick to land ball in five-metre area outside the 22-m line. E collects balls. When all players have kicked they change to a position outside the 22-m line. E changes to the goal-line to collect kicked balls. Repeat, kicking to land the ball in the five-metre area close to the goal-line. Use the left foot when kicking from the goal-line and right foot from the 22-m line.

Up-and-under practice — Each player except E has a ball. E is in a position about 20 metres out to receive the players' up-and-unders.

A kicks a high up-and-under to E and then sprints forward to attempt to touch him as he is taking the ball. Change catchers.

Coaching and Team Analysis

The coach must define success for his team and then work towards achieving it. He must devise a team pattern that his players are capable of implementing, as it is pointless to attempt sophisticated ploys if the team is not skilled or confident enough to carry them through. It is better to do a few elementary things well, practise them, and build the game around them. As the year goes on other drills and skills can be added to the pattern. Players enjoy this building process, and it can make practice sessions meaningful and progressive — something that becomes more necessary and more difficult as the year wears on.

To achieve an effective pattern the coach must understand the game itself, and be ready to accept new thinking and to divorce himself from long-held ideas. At every game he must watch his team rather than the game. It is important that the coach be able to recall as much of the game as possible, so that aspects of it and incidents in it can be discussed with players afterwards and during subsequent practices.

Coaching Ethics

It is very important that the coach adopt a professional attitude towards his team. He should never be guilty of discussing any member of his team in a derogatory manner with anyone else — particularly with other members of the team. Certainly, failings and weaknesses of individuals and the team should be discussed in a stimulating and helpful way at team sessions, but the team spirit should ensure that this is not going to drain the confidence of individuals or upset them personally. Running down players in discussions with others (players, officials, etc.,) is thoroughly unprofessional.

The coach must come to grips with behaviour problems in his team. He must set standards of behaviour, language, drink, etc., and be prepared to enforce them. His own behaviour must be exemplary, and at all times he must create the image of being a suitable person to be in charge of players. It is particularly important that he project this image to parents and supporters.

Team Analysis

Perhaps the most difficult thing for a coach to do is to diagnose his team's strengths and weaknesses and remedy the faults. It is easy to see a fault, but more difficult to know what caused it and then to put it right.

There is always a tendency in watching the game to follow the ball and miss out on the rest of the action. It is easy to become caught up in the game and enjoy the entertainment, but a coach should have self-discipline and be able to survey any one part of the game at any time. It is impossible to remember every important occurrence on the field, and therefore it is essential to take notes for future reference and analysis.

Game Analysis Card

Use a ✓ to indicate lineouts etc. for your side and a ✗ to indicate against. Use players' initials under their number.

			1	2	3	4	5	6	7	8	9	10	11	12	13	14	15	R	R
A		KICKS																	
B		TACKLING																	
C		PASSING																	
D		POSITION & SUPPORT																	
E		SKILLS Sidestep Bump																	
F	1st Half	LINEOUTS For Ag																	
G		SCRUMS For Ag																	
H		MAULS For Ag																	
I		RUCKS For Ag																	
J	2nd Half	LINEOUTS For Ag																	
K		SCRUMS For Ag																	
L		MAULS For Ag																	
M		RUCKS For Ag																	
		SCORE:																	

Sample Training Session (during the playing season)

All training sessions should start and finish punctually at a pre-arranged time. A good coach sets an example by being changed and on the ground ready to begin work at an appointed time.

	SAMPLE 1	*SAMPLE 2*
INTRODUCTORY	(a) Basic set of six stretching exercises (b) Pyramid run (c) Shuttle run (d) Circuit training	(a) Stretching — any set of six (b) Stamina (c) 12 minutes run (d) Free practice with balls
STRENGTH AND CONTACT	(a) Step-ups (b) Short wheel-barrows (c) Chinese get-up (d) Smuggle the ball	(a) Hip lift (b) One-handed tug-of-wars (c) Two-man scrum (d) Four-man rowing
TEACHING INDIVIDUAL SKILLS THEN PRACTICE THROUGH MINI GAMES	(a) Kicking: punting the ball (b) In pairs (c) Keep then run Relay (d) Throw or kick and run	(a) Catching (b) Number ball (c) Keep then run ball moving (d) High Ball
UNIT SKILLS	**Backs:** Blind side from scrums — attack and defence **Forwards:** Scrum machine (30-60 scrums)	**Backs:** Defensive from lineouts. Box kicks and grubber kicks. **Forwards:** Mauling: use tackle bags for resistance
TEAM RUN	Attacking and defensive routines from scrums	Touch rugby: backs v. forwards

A Five-Minute Guide to the Rules

by Derek Robinson
(From *Instant Rugby* by Derek Robinson, published by the Rugby Football Union, and reproduced with permission)

The law book – *Laws of the Game of Rugby Football* – is not the easiest to read or understand, but if you commit to memory the guidelines given here you will have a very reasonable understanding of the basic points.

Off-side

The off-side law for open play is not the same as that for scrums, rucks, mauls and line-outs. *In open play* you are off-side when you are in front of a player on your own team who has the ball or who has last played it. Being off-side means you're out of the game and you must not take part in it *in any way* until you are put on-side again. There is nothing wrong in being off-side. Every player is bound to be off-side at some point in the game. You get penalised only when you're off-side *and you try to take part in the game.*

• Remember: simply being in front of the ball does not make you off-side. You are only off-side if you are in front of the ball *when your team has it (or in front of the last man in your team to play it)* and you haven't been put on-side again.

If you're off-side when a player on your team kicks ahead, and you're within ten metres of an opponent *waiting for the ball,* you must clear off fast until you're ten metres from him, or you'll be penalised. Just by staying near him you are affecting the game. You must retire at once; nothing he may do can put you on-side.

On-side means you are no longer off-side, so you can take part in the game again. Any off-side player (including one off-side under the 'Ten-Metre' Law *and retiring*) can be put on-side *by his own team* in these four ways:

1. A team-mate who kicked the ball when behind him now runs in front of him.
2. Any other team-mate who was on-side when the ball was kicked now runs in front of him.
3. A team-mate with the ball runs in front of him.
4. He runs behind any of these team-mates.

Any off-side player (*except* one off-side under the 'Ten-Metre' Law) is put on-side if *an opponent* does one of these things:

1. carries the ball five metres;
2. kicks or passes the ball;
3. intentionally touches it but doesn't hold it.

Except where the 'Ten-Metre' Law applies, any

player who is off-side in open play is *always* put on-side the moment an opponent kicks, passes or deliberately touches the ball.

Off-side at a line-out. *For players taking part in a line-out:* (i.e. all forwards, both scrum-halves, the player throwing in, his opposite number) – until the ball has touched a player or the ground, the off-side line is the line-of-touch. After that, the off-side line runs through the ball itself. If you're in a line-out, keep on your side of the line until the ball arrives. Then keep on your side of the ball until the line-out ends.

For players not taking part in a line-out: (i.e. all remaining backs) – the off-side line is ten metres behind the line-of-touch, or the goal-line, whichever is nearer. Until the line-out ends, stay behind that line.

When the line-out starts and ends: A line-out starts when the ball leaves the hands of the player throwing in. It ends when one of four things happens:

1. The ball leaves the line-out.

2. A player carrying the ball leaves the line-out.

3. The ball is thrown beyond the furthest player in the line-out.

4. A ruck or maul forms and the entire ruck or maul has moved beyond the line-of-touch.

Ruck and maul off-side—In a ruck (ball on ground) or a maul (ball being carried) the off-side is like the one for a scrum: it runs through the tail-end of the ruck or maul. If you're not in a ruck or maul, you must *either* get stuck in on your own side, behind the ball, *or* get back behind your off-side line.

Scrum off-side—For everyone except scrum-halves, the off-side line runs through the tail-end of the scrum. Any player not in the scrum must stay behind this line until the ball comes out. Players in the scrum (and that means *binding*) can leave it before the ball does, as long as they retreat behind the off-side line. Scrum-halves must stay behind the ball until it's out.

Scrums and mauls: get in them
or get behind them
but don't just hang around them

Don't handle the ball in a scrum.
Don't make the scrum collapse.
Don't kick the ball out of the tunnel.
Don't put the ball back into the scrum once it's out.
Do form a scrum quickly. Form it where the ref says. Put the ball in as soon as you can after the front rows meet. Keep the tunnel clear and let the ball in.

The tackle

The tackle law has been changed.
The old law said that a player was tackled when he was held so that the ball touched the ground.

The new law says that a player is tackled when he is held and brought to ground, or held so that the ball touches the ground. 'Brought to ground' means he's not on his feet.

When you've *been* tackled, let go of the ball *at*

once, and either get away from it or get up. Leave it alone until you're on your feet.

When you've *made* a tackle, let him release the ball, and leave it alone until you're on your feet, too.

• A player can be brought down without being tackled. For instance, he might get knocked over and not held. In that case he need not let go the ball – as long as he gets back on his feet *at once.*

BANNED!

NO head high tackles

To tackle a player, you must grab him by the shoulders or below. A tackle around the neck or head is dangerous and illegal.

NO flying wedge

The flying wedge has been banned because it's dangerous. (A flying wedge is a short-range attack by linked players who try to force the ball-carrier over the goal-line.)

Advantage

If one side does something wrong, and their opponents gain an advantage from it, the game goes on without stopping. The advantage can be tactical (good attacking opportunity) or territorial (a gain in ground).

First example: A player gives a forward pass, but an opponent intercepts it and starts an attacking passing movement. He has taken tactical advantage, so the referee ignores the forward pass.

Second example: A player knocks-on and drops the

ball. His opponents kick it ahead and follow up. They have gained a territorial advantage from the knock-on, so the referee lets it pass. Advantage covers 99% of Rugby. It covers all kinds of off-side, as well as knock-ons, forward passes, scrums, rucks, mauls, line-outs, drop-outs, and in-goal play.

If you see an advantage, grab it! Never wait for the whistle.

In-goal play

All laws apply to the in-goal except tackle, scrum, maul and line-out, which apply only to the field-of-play. If a defender breaks a law in his own in-goal, a five-metre scrum is given. If an attacker breaks a law in his opponents' in-goal, a drop-out is given.

If a defender puts the ball into his own in-goal and it's made dead by *any* player, a five-metre scrum is given.

If an attacker puts the ball into his opponents' in-goal, and it's made dead by *any* player, a drop-out is given. ('Made dead' here doesn't include scoring a try.)

Lying on the ball

Falling on the ball stops a foot-rush, and is all right. Lying on the ball stops the entire game, and is all wrong.

When you fall on the ball, you must *at once* do something about it. You must *either* play the ball in some way *or* get away from it. That applies to lying *near* the ball, too.

Whatever you do, do it *at once*. Keep the game going.

Knock-on and throw forward

The only way to gain ground is to run or kick. You must not throw or knock the ball forward.

When you give a pass, the ball must go along or behind a line parallel to the goal-lines.

'Forward' does *not* mean in front of *you*. 'Forward' means towards your opponents' in-goal. If you fumble the ball and it bounces towards your own in-goal, this is not a knock-on.

Knock-on exceptions:

If a player charges down an opponent's kick (without trying to catch the ball), this is not a knock-on.

If a player knocks-on but recovers the ball before it has touched the ground or another player, this is not a knock-on.

- **It's an offence to knock the ball forward intentionally, even if you catch it again.**

10-a-side Rugby

Ten-a-side rugby contains the main elements of the national 15-a-side game—running, passing, catching, tackling and backing up — but by reducing the number of players in the team players become much more involved. And this greater involvement can, for a lot of players, mean greater enjoyment.

Rules of the game

A 10-a-side team has five forwards and five backs. Three form the front row and two the second row at all scrums, and there are not less than four players at every lineout. Behind the scrum there is a scrum-half, five-eighth, centre, wing and fullback.

The game is played 12 minutes each way with up to five minutes at halftime. If a player is injured during the game and has to leave the field, a replacement player is allowed to join the game. No more than two replacements are allowed per game. All of the normal rugby rules apply as usual, except that all kicks at goal must be drop-kicks.

In the event of a draw at fulltime, a one-versus-one instant play-off takes place. The best total from the five players' efforts — from first one team then the other — decides the winner. If the result is still a draw, then turns are alternated with other members. The first to score points wins. In each case, a coin is tossed to decide the attacker and defender.

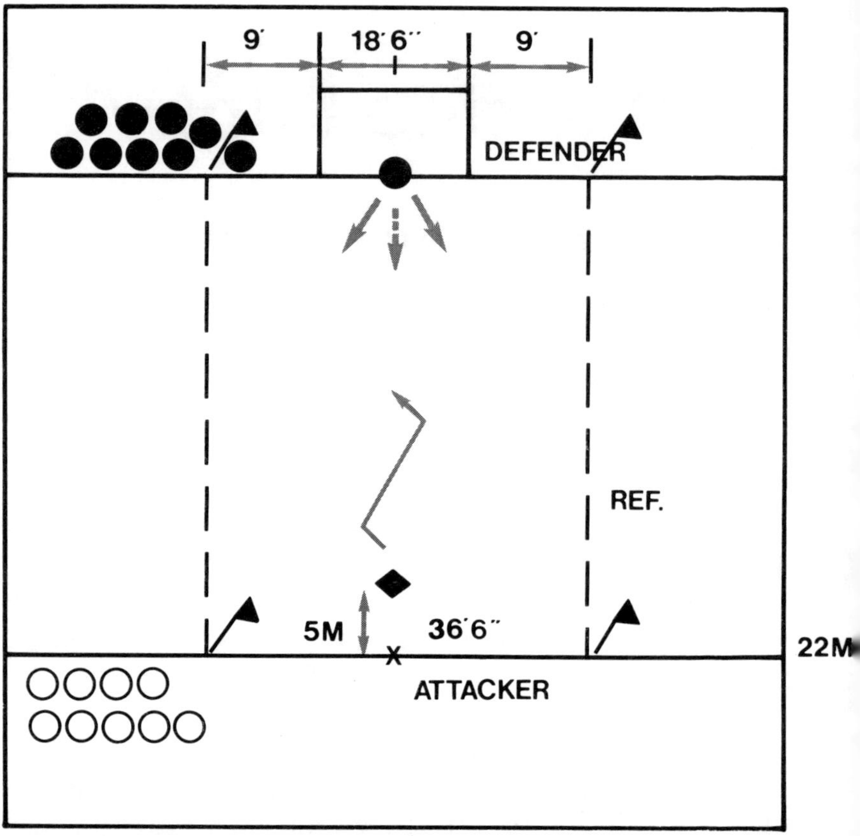

The one-versus-one instant play-off is performed as follows: The attacker stands on the 22-m line and the chosen defender between the goal posts. The ball is placed five metres in from the 22-m line. On the whistle the attacker runs, picks up the ball and tries to score a try or drop goal keeping within the defined area. Three points are awarded for a drop kick and four points for a try between the posts. Normal rugby laws apply. Any infringement and a 'no contest' is declared. The referee's decision is final. The attacker is out of the contest when tackled with the ball to the ground. (Points from a play-off do not count towards a final table if playing in a tournament.)

tries are equal, a coin is tossed.

If in a tournament two or more teams are equal on points at the end of the round, then the first two places are determined by (in this order):

(a) Which of the teams wins the game(s) played against each other.

(b) The greatest number of tries scored.

(c) The points for and against over the whole round.

(d) Tossing a coin.

Appendix One
A few facts about the human body

When the body is at rest the heart pumps out about five litres of blood every minute, and five to eight litres of air are inhaled by the lungs. The human body is built for action, not rest. During activity the heart is capable of pumping about 20 litres of blood every minute, and 100 litres of air are inhaled by the lungs.

Our heart beats about 70 times a minute. It pumps blood via pulmonary arteries to the lungs where it is oxygenated, then via the aorta to all parts of the body. As we do more work or run harder, more blood is pumped by the heart.

The heart rates for the average person in various activities are:

- Lying down .... about 70 beats per minute
- Walk around .... about 90 beats per minute
- Slow jog .... about 110 beats per minute
- Run .... about 140 beats per minute

With the right type of activity you can lower your heart rate, but have more oxygenated blood pumped around your body. A fit person would have a heart beat of about 45 beats per minute lying down and increase accordingly.

Appendix Two
The rugby ground and ball

The accompanying diagram shows the recommended dimensions of the field-of-play and of the goal. Broken lines (———) indicate 10 metres distance from the

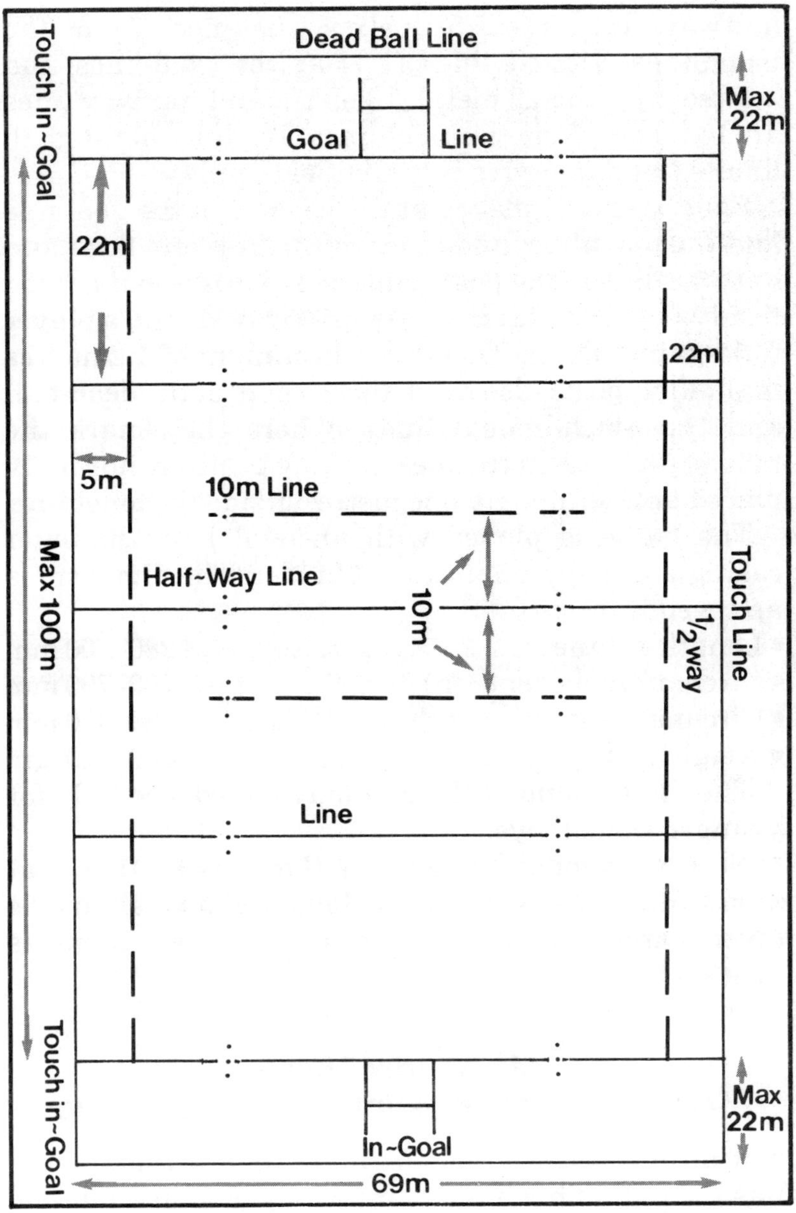
Dead Ball Line
Touch in~Goal
Max 22m
Goal Line
22m
22m
5m
10m Line
Half~Way Line
10m
Max 100m
Touch Line
1/2 way
Line
Touch in~Goal
Max 22m
In~Goal
69m

halfway line and 5 metres distance from the touchlines. Dotted lines (...) at the goal-lines and intersecting the 22-metre, 10-metre and halfway lines are 15 metres from the touchlines. The lines at the goal-lines extend 5 metres into the field-of-play.

Flag posts are placed at the corners of the goal-line and the touchline, and to mark the 22-metre lines and halfway lines. The posts should be upright but not too firmly fixed, so that they will give way should a player fall against them. They are a minimum of 1.2 metres high. Flag posts also mark the corners of the dead-ball and the touch-in-goal lines. Where they mark the halfway and 22-metre lines, the flag posts are normally placed approximately one metre outside the touchline.

The game is played with an oval ball, the outer casing enclosing an inflated bladder. The dimensions and weight are:

- Length in line .... 280–300 mm
- Circumference (end on)................ 760–790 mm
- Circumference (in width) .... 580–620 mm
- Weight................................. 400–440 gm

The dimensions of the ball may be reduced only for younger schoolboys.

Nothing should be used in the construction that might injure the players. The lacing, if any, should be given careful attention so that the outer casing is neatly closed.

Appendix Three
Some interesting points about the game

- In an 80-minute game of rugby the average player has the ball in his hands for no longer than a minute.

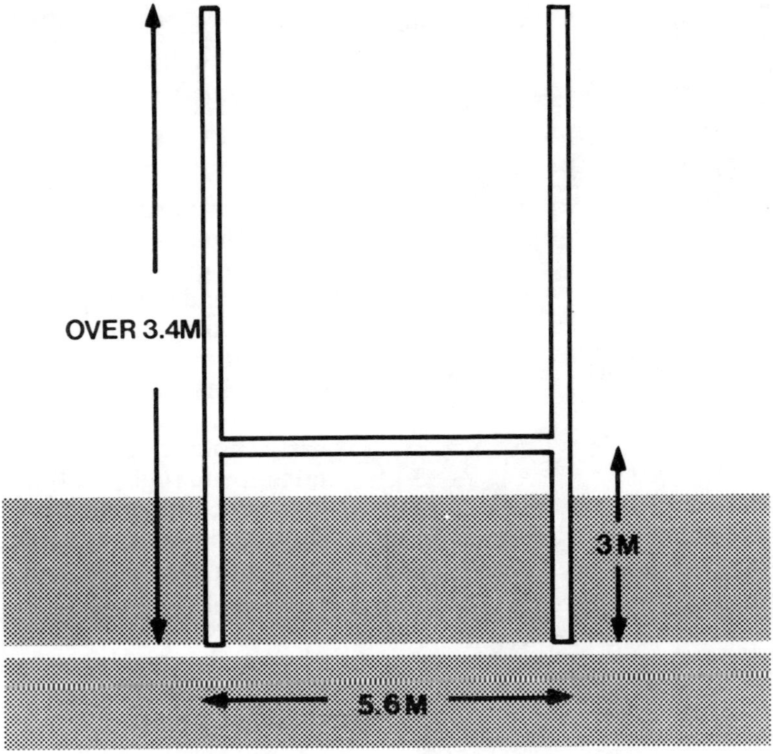

- On an average there are 44 lineouts in a game.
- Scrums usually total 52 per game.
- Rucks and mauls average 38 per game.
- Actual running time is 27 minutes per game.
- Forwards cover about 5200 metres or 15 laps of playing field, and backs cover 3600 metres or 11 laps of playing field.
- Forwards cover one third of the distance at top speed, and the backs cover half of their running distance at top pace.